When Will It Happen For Me?

A Shame-Free Guide
to Finding Love
On Your Own Timeline

When Will It Happen For Me?

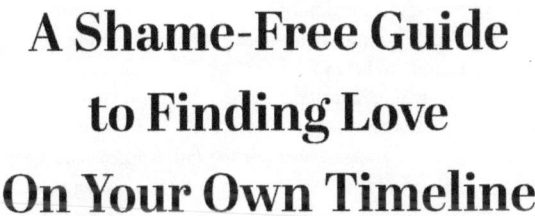

A Shame-Free Guide
to Finding Love
On Your Own Timeline

PHOEBE ROGERS

First published by The Kind Press in 2025
Copyright © Phoebe Rogers 2025

All rights reserved. No part of this book may be reproduced by any mechanical, photographic or electronic process, including AI-generated reproductions, or in the form of a phonographic recording, nor may it be stored in a retrieval system, transmitted, or otherwise copied for public or private use other than for 'fair use' as brief quotations embodied in articles and reviews without prior written permission from the publisher.

Cover design: by Christa Moffitt, Christabella Designs
Author photo credit: Jade Warne
Typeset in 12/17 pt Minion 3 by Post Pre-press Group

 A catalogue record for this book is available from the National Library of Australia

ISBN: 9781763800908 (paperback)
ISBN: 9781763800922 (eBook)

This book is provided for informational purposes only and is not intended as a substitute for psychological, financial, legal or professional advice. The intent of the author is only to offer information of a general nature to help you in your quest for emotional, physical and spiritual wellbeing, however, individual circumstances vary. Readers should seek guidance from appropriately qualified professionals where necessary. In the event you use any of the information in this book for yourself, neither the publisher nor the author accepts any liability for any loss, damage or disruption arising from reliance on the information contained in this book. This includes but is not limited to direct, indirect, incidental, special or consequential damages. By engaging with this material, readers acknowledge personal responsibility for their own choices and actions.

The Kind Press acknowledges the Traditional Owners of Country throughout Australia and acknowledges their continuing connection to land, waters and community. We pay our respects to the people, the cultures and the Elders past and present.

For women everywhere—
longing for love

Most of all, to J—
for showing me how true love feels

Contents

Introduction: Another Breakup, A Breakthrough — 1

PART ONE Rebuilding After a Breakup
Chapter One: First You Must Grieve — 11
Chapter Two: The Love Stories We Inherit — 23
Chapter Three: Rediscovering Your Old Self — 37
Chapter Four: The Upside of Anger — 49

PART TWO Repatterning For Love
Chapter Five: Healing Your Wounds — 61
Chapter Six: Core Skills That Heal — 73
Chapter Seven: Attachment is Everything — 87
Chapter Eight: The Shame That Lurks Within — 99

PART THREE Seeking Love
Chapter Nine: Dating With Eyes Wide Open — 115
Chapter Ten: How To Choose A Long-Term Partner — 127
Chapter Eleven: What Do You Want From Love? — 139
Chapter Twelve: Letting Love In — 151

PART FOUR Building Security In Love

Chapter Thirteen: Being A Grown Up In Love	167
Chapter Fourteen: The Hiccups of Healing	179
Chapter Fifteen: Momentum and Milestones	189
Chapter Sixteen: Moving In	201
Chapter Seventeen: Separateness Versus Togetherness	213
Chapter Eighteen: Starting Over (Again)	221
Epilogue: Love Isn't Perfect	233
Appendix: Extra Resources	237
Acknowledgements	243
About the author	245

INTRODUCTION

Another Breakup, A Breakthrough

It's a very vulnerable feeling to be a couples therapist who can't find love. To sit across the room from a couple in distress that are desperately longing to reconnect and fall in love again, when you have struggled with that very thing too. When, perhaps, you've never had a healthy relationship yourself; when you so deeply long for love; when you wonder if, for you, it's ever going to happen.

It's a very vulnerable feeling to be a couples therapist who has just called off her engagement, wondering if the couples in your clinic will begin to notice the missing diamond ring on your finger. To tear up in session more often than seems normal for a therapist, because you are listening to stories of love and loss, and it resonates so deeply and hurts your heart.

It's a very vulnerable feeling to be a couples therapist who has lost hope in finding love for herself; to be in a world of pain masked to the outside world, and to still show up for others in their quest for love. Because one thing that is true of me is that I will always show up for anyone's quest for love. That's how much I strongly believe in love. That's how much I want others, and women in particular, to find the kind of love they deserve to experience.

The period of my life which inspired this book began when I was thirty-six years old. I had just started working for myself in my private practice as a Clinical Psychologist and couples therapist and I was good at it. I could, and still do, change the lives of my clients. I have the insight and ability to transform your relationship landscape. But, whilst my inner-city Sydney practice was thriving, my personal life was falling apart. There, behind my warm and comforting smile and my professional wisdom, laid a deep, dark pain, and a feeling of emptiness.

Over the next eighteen chapters, you'll learn more about my story but, for now, I'll give you the movie-plot breakdown. In 2021, I found myself unexpectedly single once again. To be honest, it probably wasn't too unexpected. Another failed relationship, with similar themes to the others before that: exhaustion, fatigue, emptiness and a real loss of myself. Two years earlier, during the confusion of the pandemic, I had met a kindred spirit on a dating app, or so I thought. In hindsight, the red flags were there (I'll share these later, don't worry!). Within nineteen months, I was done. I was sick of fighting, sick of hurting, and sick of him and how I felt around him. I was absolutely walking on eggshells. It was only the year before that we had met, and life felt so incredibly blissful. I thought this was different, that I had finally found my person, someone to love me for who I am. It felt special, magical, 'meant to be'.

When I called off our engagement, I knew it was the right decision, but it didn't make it any easier to digest, even with my professional background. When you end a relationship, even for the right reasons, it's a confusing medley of relief, despair, loneliness and euphoria.

Introduction

I remember a photo of myself on my 36th birthday, shortly after the breakup. I was now living alone in an apartment that used to be ours. It was peaceful and quiet, spacious, modern, and all mine. I felt both aching and relief. In the photo I was sitting at the dining table, looking out through the windows that let in so much light, the trees and city view. I could hardly be bothered to dress, opting for a simple t-shirt and trackpants. My ex-fiancé had just visited and brought me a chocolate cake with candles, which I both wanted and didn't want from him.

I didn't want to be alone on my birthday, yet I didn't really want him there either. In the photo I have a big, warm, happy smile on my face. In reality, I had just been crying, totally gutted that I would be single and alone again. That was my truth for some time. Behind my ever-present smile was such hurt and loneliness. I really wanted to have it all figured out by now. I really wanted to be in love; to have found my person. Don't most of us want that?

For me, this breakup was especially complex as I was experiencing it both personally and professionally. I could experience it from my heart—as the person who was alone and suffering—and from my head, as a psychologist who could join the dots between my past and my present problems. And, I knew there had to be a better way...

So after this final breakup, that was equal parts despairing and liberating, I made a vow to myself—to never, ever find myself in a dysfunctional, unhappy relationship ever again. And, most of all, I made a vow to never, ever lose myself in a relationship again. There's just some things one should never do, even for love. I never wanted to forget who I was or stop doing the things that brought me joy. I never wanted to find myself in a place where I couldn't freely express my thoughts, ideas, feelings, opinions, beliefs and needs for fear of conflict. I never wanted my boundaries to be violated. This vow felt like a crystal-clear breakthrough. I was going to rebuild my life, rediscover myself, and find love. However, it had to be very different than before.

This book is all about how I became my own case study—how I approached my own love life like I would the problems of the clients who come into my clinic. Because, I hadn't really done this before. We all know, it can be hard to take our own advice. Plus, as someone working in a caring profession, it can be easy to get Compassion Fatigue—with yourself. I had so much empathy and understanding and wisdom when it came to my clients. And so much empathy for my own broken heart. Imagine if I could tap into that source for my own romantic development.

And so, in August 2021, alone in my apartment, I decided to go on a big journey of self to figure all this messy stuff out. I had done therapy before, and had learnt a lot about relationships, and treating my own depression, however, I needed something more. I had an unshakeable inner sense that I needed to heal my past relationship wounds once and for all. I also needed to find someone who could help me truly understand how a healthy love feels, could guide me in how to know love when I find it, and how to actively cultivate love with a romantic partner. I needed to figure out how to manage all my anxiety around relationships, how to cope with my fear of abandonment and managing a partner's distance. And I needed to trust in my worth, my value, my goodness, and believe that there was someone out there who could see and love those parts of me too.

Did I find love? You'll have to read on to find out. That isn't really the point of this story, even if it's a big part of our inner narrative. We are conditioned especially as women, to think that

Introduction

finding 'true love' will be our happiest ending. There is, however, an amazing level of happiness, connection and intimacy that you can find on the healing journey, long before you meet the person or people of your dreams.

The Self-Love Formula

I started this chapter by saying, it's a vulnerable feeling to be a couples therapist who can't find love, and that is true. But it isn't a shameful place to be. This book, and my work, is a judgement-free and shame-free space. This is the truth of my story, and it is one that I choose to no longer feel ashamed of because it has put me on a path of healing and self-knowledge that is empowering.

I am truly grateful to my past. Through my own courage to face my past and heal, I now deeply know what it takes to find love and keep love alive. My story has been filled with bleakness, periods of depression, intense loneliness, shame, and yearning for love. However, it is also a story of courage, hope, and vulnerability, complete with my very own happy ever after, and that's why I feel called to share this story with you. It is a story of going deep within your heart, doing the work, healing, and becoming a more resilient and empowered version of you. Most of all, it is a story of love. A story of loving yourself more than ever, and showing up as your most authentic self each and every day. Because when you meet your person, you will know in your soul that they choose the real you, flaws and all. I want to show you how I got there, so you too can find love. The type of love that is deep, accepting, secure and has strong roots. I want to help you find love by knowing the path to take you there.

When Will It Happen For Me

This book is for you if:

- ♥ You've had enough of choosing partners who are emotionally unavailable and lack security in themselves, and a sense of life direction and purpose
- ♥ You've had enough of choosing partners who need you but don't give to you
- ♥ You've had enough of excessively giving to and taking care of a partner to the detriment of your emotional wellbeing
- ♥ You've had enough of getting hurt, and becoming burnt out and resentful because that is not a healthy relationship energy
- ♥ You're frustrated that you don't have love all figured out and fear you may be alone forever

I felt like that … and I'm a professional!

To be clear, this story isn't about blaming others, it is about understanding and letting go. Whilst the things that happened to us in early life are not our fault, they are ours to work on. I have compassion and understanding for all humans because we all inherit a lot of messy stuff to work through. I believe it is our own responsibility to fix our stuff, and in doing so, we can come closer to happiness and have more deeply connected and intimate love stories.

Throughout this book, I want to share with every single woman, whether single or partnered, what I learnt from my journey of dating, therapy, reading self-help books, and healing. There are answers, and there is a formula as such. I want to share with you the work I am currently doing that is informed by my own healing and is currently helping women find the love that they long for.

Introduction

I run a successful women's group therapy program online that teaches women all the relationship skills that are also in this book. I continue to be floored by the courage and vulnerability I witness as they heal. For the first time in my life, I am crystal clear on the steps needed to heal, so that you can find and maintain a healthy love. I truly believe if you follow the wisdom in this book, you too can have your happy ever after. My healing journey helped me cultivate a truly healthy and happy relationship with myself and opened the door to the possibility of a truly healthy relationship with a partner. I want this for all of womankind.

This book is for women much like myself: smart, hardworking, kind, and knowing deep down that they long for a relationship. This book is for the single woman who has a deep yearning in her heart for her soulmate, it is for the woman who is questioning jumping off the dating apps after one too many disappointments, and it is for the woman who is newly dating yet filled with anxiety that she's going to end up rejected or abandoned. This book is also for the woman who wants more feeling and intimacy in her current relationship, the one who holds back for fear she is too emotional or won't get her needs met. This book is for any woman who wants more romance, more confidence, and a secure love in her life. This book will teach you skills in clarifying your relationship values, developing standards and healthy boundaries for your relationships, identifying red flags, assessing for emotional maturity in a partner, soothing your anxiety when dating, communicating with more openness and vulnerability to increase connection, and cultivating a strong internal self-love that anchors you through the bumps of life.

If you have ever existed in an unhappy relationship and made the courageous decision to leave, I applaud you. And if you've ever been left suddenly and shockingly, the rug pulled out from underneath you, I understand that pain. I have lived through the pain of leaving, and the pain of being left, and both hurt like hell. I want to show you how to connect with your grief to support your growth and healing. I want to equip you for the next wonderful chapter of your life.

May this book serve as a guide book for healing; a roadmap on all things love, whether it be finding the right partner, or deepening the love you have with your current partner. This guide can be used at any stage of your relationship journey. There are therapeutic exercises in each chapter to support you and help you develop insight and skills along your healing journey. Above all, it is my wish that this book brings you hope and optimism about love. It is out there waiting for you! Let's get to finding it.

With so much love, Phoebe.

PART ONE

Rebuilding After a Breakup

CHAPTER ONE
First You Must Grieve

It was the beginning of the pandemic, early 2020, and I had been feeling alone and disconnected from the world. So, I did what any single woman in Sydney struggling would do and got on to an online dating app. Thanks to the wonders of technology, two souls found each other during troubling times. Are you seeing the red flags already? I was an ambitious but disconnected professional who had been looking for love for fifteen years. The guy I matched with, and met, was in his mid-thirties, had been single for years, and lived with his extended family. He kept a small circle and felt equally disconnected to others. Yet he seemed very interested and curious about me. From our first meeting, we were inseparable.

He brought me flowers and gifts, cooked for me, and I felt nurtured and at home. He seemed to treasure me from the moment we met. When he proposed to me two months after we met, I said 'yes' without hesitation. Suddenly, I was planning a wedding to a man that I hardly knew, and it was gaining momentum. I thought the intensity of it was normal because we were 'meant to be', and now I look back and wonder if I was simply 'love bombed'.

When Will It Happen For Me

Much of that time of my life was a blur. What I will never forget however, are the clear memories of visualising my wedding day on repeat. This is when I'd be most crippled with anxiety. I'd imagine myself getting ready on my wedding day or walking down the aisle in the most perfect whimsical dress, eventually meeting my groom and saying 'yes'. I imagined I'd get all the way to that point and want to run. Alarm bells went off inside my body anytime I thought about these moments; a feeling of dread deep in the pit of my stomach at the prospect of saying 'yes' to a life sentence of unhappiness.

Of course, as a couples counsellor, I knew this was not a good sign. But the self-protection of denial is strong. Yes, I questioned if this was really how a woman should feel about spending the rest of her life with a partner. When he talked about our wedding day, I wondered if he truly knew the size of my own doubts. I wondered if he thought this was how we should be getting along before our wedding. But it was so easy to get caught up in the momentum, especially once we told our friends and family. My parents were always supportive of me, however, as my distress became more obvious, I recall mum asking me if I really felt he was 'the one' for me, and I remember my dad expressing concerns about how I was being treated. My protective dad didn't want me to take too much blame for things, and cautioned that my partner needed to work on himself rather than us going to couples therapy. Looking back, it was like everyone could see the trainwreck happening from the outside. And, yet every time I felt doubts, they were overshadowed by the voice in my head which said:

At least he loves you.
A least someone loves you.

How I ended up leaving that relationship matters less than what happened afterwards. Let's just say, I could've so easily said 'yes' to a lifetime of entrapment. I thank that quiet voice within me that grew louder and more outraged at the idea of settling for something that didn't feel right. I stayed in that relationship longer than was necessary in order to avoid the pain of being alone.

Now I can see, my urge to not be alone and longing to be truly loved, propelled me down a path of failed relationships again and again, and would have continued to if I didn't address it properly this time. We, as women, experience a collective pain and grief that, if not addressed, can impact every aspect of our life. So, let's talk about it ...

Starting Young: Our Search for Love

I have come to observe a clear pattern in my work as a Clinical Psychologist and couples therapist that unfortunately not all of us are set up to truly know what a healthy love is as a result of early life events. I believe that whilst this is true for all genders and sexual orientations, it has a particular pattern in women and those socialised as women. Women have been taught to give love, but are not very good at receiving love or truly believing that they deserve to receive from love. You may, indeed, relate to some of these feelings.

These are just some of the patterns of love I've observed in my female clients. They:

- ♥ Grew up feeling that they were worthwhile because they were kind, patient, giving and empathic

When Will It Happen For Me

- ♥ Grew up making themselves small; conscious of not burdening others or asking for or expecting too much in an already overwhelmed and stressed family system
- ♥ Grew up with self-sacrificing mothers who served their family and nurtured others, and failed to model the importance of nurturing themselves
- ♥ Observed their mothers living in unhappy and emotionally unfulfilling relationships that diminished their confidence and sense of self-worth
- ♥ Have been taught to not upset others, to walk on eggshells around a moody parent or sibling
- ♥ Have been taught to not complain or get angry
- ♥ Feel like their emotions are too much, that they are too needy, that they should just be happy and grateful with whatever they get
- ♥ Grew up being praised and rewarded for their empathy, for their quiet introversion, for not stealing the spotlight off others; and
- ♥ Many, many of my female clients have experienced being shamed for showing their vulnerability, or expressing anxiety, worry and sadness when in fact it is appropriate and shows their humanity

With these early life events, is it any wonder that we have found ourselves in relationships that lack fairness and reciprocity, and result in hurt and pain?

The Pain We Bypass

Let me talk a bit about the pain that us women try to bypass. In my professional life providing therapy to women for their relationships, I work in a consulting space that I hope feels welcoming and homely. You'll find pastel pink cushions and a green rug placed delicately over a lounge for individuals or couples clients. There's a window that allows in lots of warm natural light, and underneath it is a wooden side table with water and a box of tissues. Therapy essentials. And so many times, the woman in pain sitting across from me on the lounge will reach for a tissue and apologise for crying.

Picture a thirty-something-year-old woman in deep sorrow, tears streaming down her face because her heart has been recently broken. She's been joltingly left by her shutdown and withdrawing male partner of several years, and is in disbelief at the sudden ending of her relationship with the one she deeply loved and saw her life with. The one she thought she would share the rest of her days with. Picture her struggling to express words through her tears as she tells me of the confusion, shock and physical pain she is feeling, and then saying sorry for crying. She will then also question why she is still feeling this way after only several months, as if it is not normal to be feeling this way for so long. She is a woman like many of us who shame ourselves for our feelings and vulnerability, even when they are so very called for. She is a woman who like many others questions the validity of her emotions, and has lost trust in her intuition.

How many of my own therapy sessions where I am in the client chair have I cried in? Nearly all if I'm being honest. I'm a crier. I want you to know that your tears are necessary for your healing, and that the way through the heartbreak, sadness and grief is by feeling it. In fact, there is a hanging picture on the wall of my consulting room that reads 'feel so you can heal'. It's there for a reason, so please do not rush this step. You must open up your heart, turn your attention inwards and tune into your body, and notice what is happening inside. Our emotions are these wonderful messengers from inside that I believe offer so much wisdom if we listen and get curious about them, rather than avoiding them and doing whatever we can to tune them out whether with binge-watching TV, excessive food, alcohol or work.

If you've just come out of a relationship or haven't faced the sadness, disappointment, guilt, shame or self-blame of your past romantic relationship losses, you must face these feelings. You must actually feel your pain, allow yourself to sit with your emotions and have it expressed in a way that resonates for you. The only way through your pain is through it, as was true of this client's story:

I had worked with a client for several years to help her express herself in her relationship, and things seemed to be progressing well. She and her partner were making plans to move in together at last. He had expressed previous anxiety about moving forward a year before, but things seemed truly good for them both now. Just as they were ready to move in, he let her know he couldn't continue the relationship. The rug was truly pulled out from underneath her. The future that was around the corner for her, was cruelly taken away from her. And so, our work across several months was simply sitting with her pain and validating it. There were no shortcuts. I reminded her that it was going to hurt, and that I trusted in her capacity to feel it.

If you are experiencing a relationship breakdown currently, start gently, and check in with your body each day. Observe any

Rebuilding After a Breakup

feelings inside your body and ask that part of you what it needs. It probably needs warmth and compassion and presence, rather than the pain being avoided. Whether you are fresh out of a breakup or some months down the track, don't bypass this step. You must grieve. You must experience being in touch with and being moved by your own pain, so that you can feel with you and for you. What I mean by that is that you physiologically and emotionally feel care, nurturing, warmth and empathy from your heart and soul for your own relationship journey. You must be the one who understands and sees your hurt, and offers comfort to the sadness of loss.

There is so much grief when we consider love and the breakdown of a relationship. There is grief about the relationship itself, especially if you are still in love with that person (and even if you aren't). Even if you have ended the relationship and you know that it is the right thing, I give you absolute permission to be missing your ex, or the life that you had together. I give you permission to still love them or parts of them, even if they hurt you. I give you permission to grieve the loss of the life you thought you were going to have, even if parts of it didn't feel quite right anymore. Extend this permission to feel back to yourself. A relationship represents so much to each of us: a home, a sense of security, safety, connection and company, a future filled with dreams that are built on shared values. Maybe it meant someone to have your back or that you won't ever feel lost or alone in a big, scary world.

And, for some of the women I work with, a relationship represents family; to raise children, to be a mother and nurturer, and to have a beautiful impact on the world because you raise little beings with values and integrity. It is painful and pretty terrifying when your life is no longer planned out. We all have relationship dreams that we want to come true. A relationship end can feel like the death of a dream, and with death there is grief.

I had to grieve for thirty-six-year-old Phoebe who was so sad that she was alone, that she had failed at love and feared that she would be alone forever. To break up with a partner was scary because of the impending loneliness which I dreaded. I felt alone and misunderstood, and that was the pain that hurt the most. I felt isolated, and as if no one could understand the gravity of the situation: I'd just called off a wedding, and I was thirty-six and destined for a future of uncertainty. I suspect I felt my own shame, and also the shame that comes from familial and societal expectations about the natural order of life for a woman. I needed to be understood, and craved empathy and comfort from others.

One of the most powerful healing lessons for me was coming to the realisation that I could be the one who understands and validates my own emotions and experiences. I could be my own shoulder to cry on through the unrelenting waves of grief. That I should not and cannot depend on others to be constant sources of empathy and validation, and this can be empowering.

Unfortunately, a common legacy of trauma and not feeling you received validation, empathy, nurturance and worth from your caregivers, is that you keep searching for it in others, particularly adult romantic partners later in life. I wanted a parent or a friend to tell me something to soothe my grief, I wanted someone to sit beside me during dark, sleepless nights and reassure me it was all going to be okay. I wanted someone to intuitively sense my pain and offer to spend time with me. And I used to believe that it was incredibly reasonable to have these expectations of others. Now, I see it as my responsibility to validate my own emotions and comfort myself, as well as ask for support when I most need it.

Rebuilding After a Breakup

I also must be kind and gracious when care is given, and often need to realise that everyone is doing their best to show care whilst balancing their own needs too. Self-validation and extending words of empathy inwards can support you through your grief. The empathy of others is a welcomed bonus.

So, how else did I grieve? To be frank, I didn't really know what I was doing, and for a psychologist, I wasn't as vulnerable or expressive as I had previously considered myself. I am much better with the feelings of others than my own. My own depression threatened to swallow me, and my anxiety and panic about my future was overwhelming at times. I did a lot of going into problem-solving mode in order not to feel. I worked, I ate a lot of chocolate, I read, I found hobbies, and I distracted myself. And then I'd burst into tears in the middle of a spin class at the gym.

What I discovered about my grief was that I should cry if particular music or love songs moved me, and I should cry under the private comfort of a hot shower. It was also okay to cry when a woman's love story moved me in session, and it is okay to self-disclose some of my own grief in session in order to take a stand against shaming women and their emotions. I have grieved by journaling and writing about all the emotions I felt about my relationship ending. I have particularly found it helpful to journal about my anger about how I was treated and allowed myself to be treated. That form of expression can free up a lot of stuck emotions because the anger moves away and clears space for the sadness underneath to be felt. Therapy was a huge part of my grieving process and allowed me to express my grief, fear, loneliness and worry for the future. I also reminded myself that these feelings were here to teach me a lesson, and that any heartbreak or loss has served me both personally and professionally.

When Will It Happen For Me

I had to learn how to soothe myself and be on my own. Do see if you can find some meaning in your suffering. As I told one of my clients who bravely ended her relationship as her partner expressed too much ambivalence about his intentions for their future: 'I promise you that your grief and emotions are guiding you towards a brighter path.' She ended a relationship that wasn't serving her, as she knew deeply in her soul that she wanted children and an emotionally available partner in her future. I had no doubt in her choice.

To the woman reading these pages, may you open your heart, feel what must be felt, find meaning in your pain, and rediscover who you truly are.

EXERCISE
Connect with Your Grief

In order to heal, you must connect with your grief. List here the emotions that arise for you when a relationship has ended. Describe where each emotion sits in your body and the sensations that are present. Try and check in with your body each day and notice what emotions are present.

EXERCISE
Validate Your Grief

You are the one who validates and nurtures your own emotions now. Write some empathic statements here to offer comfort to yourself. Imagine what you would love to hear from another at your time of need. Access your inner nurturer.

An example:

I'm so sorry you're hurting right now, and I see the distress you feel. I can understand the fear and loneliness that is coming up for you right now. Your emotions are most welcome now, and I'll be here with you at this hard time.

We will keep returning to the idea of cultivating self-nurturing.

CHAPTER TWO
The Love Stories We Inherit

When I first began my journey as a Clinical Psychologist, it was all about my fascination with the mind, people and helping others. It was informed by my father's work as a mental health nurse. I was only twenty-four-years-old when I commenced my training, had never experienced a mental illness and considered myself a well-adjusted human being. Perhaps I was a little insecure, but aren't we all? Now when I think of my age and life experience at that time, I cringe at how ill-prepared I really was to understand the depths of despair of some of the humans I met. My empathy and capacity to truly understand their misery came much later in life, after my own life fell apart.

It was several years later, at the critical age of thirty that things became much darker and I became much less naive. Life plodded along for some time with ease and general contentment. I generally thought life was good and generous, and things tended to always work out okay in the end. So you can imagine my disbelief when I first found myself in a fellow psychologist's office and I was diagnosed with depression.

When Will It Happen For Me

It was such a strange thing to be there. I knew how 'down' I was and simultaneously wrestled with accepting the idea that I—Phoebe, the psychologist—was so unwell and needed help. And I was really unwell. To the point that I questioned the point of life itself. So, how did I find myself there?

At the time, I had been in a relationship for just over a year and a half with a guy who I met online. He was my age, a university student, and had a complicated relationship with his family. He was a mix of intriguing, smart and naïve. He was incredibly introverted and seemed to prefer his own space and time. He seemed stressed and preoccupied with his studies, I was deeply longing for more connection and intimacy. I was giving a lot of myself at work and even more of myself in my relationship. This relationship just stopped being fun; in fact, it was draining my life force out of me. My partner was floundering in his own life, clearly overwhelmed by juggling his responsibilities and a new relationship which demanded things of him, such as time and energy.

I felt powerless; as if nothing I could say or do could shine any light on his gloomy outlook. I was tired, exhausted and over functioning in every aspect of that relationship. I was giving more emotional and mental resources than I was receiving or had within me. I was overextending myself, self-sacrificing and compromising in order to keep the relationship going. And I was struggling with his unhappiness and emotional withdrawal, and somehow thought that, if I was more loving, more patient, more understanding, more agreeable, and asked for less of him, that it would all be okay. Because isn't that what we've been shown to do? Give all you have until the point of depletion to make another happy.

I see this in so many of my female clients. Meanwhile, inside of me was growing a brooding anger and resentment, deep loneliness and sadness for feeling so neglected. Whilst he had emotionally neglected me, the truth was I had neglected myself. I had participated in my own demise, and that was more devastating to me. How had I developed so little regard for myself? And, because it unconsciously didn't feel safe to be angry out of fear of losing the relationship (fear of abandonment is a real thing), that anger turned inwards and festered into depression. Angry and resentful women are at huge risk of developing depression. This was just one important turning point in my story.

Sadly, this pattern repeated across several more years and several more relationships. It took me multiple downward turns to realise these patterns still repeat and can cause illness. I believe I finally broke that pattern when I called off my engagement. That was the last break that I decided I could tolerate. Whilst there is always constant self-work to do, I know now that I deeply and truly understood the lesson. The lesson of what I inherited about love, and that I needed to dedicate myself to heal once and for all.

The Wisdom of Our Wounds

Clearly my interest in psychology was more personal and profound than I first thought. I was drawn to psychology because of the wounded part of me. The Wounded Healer Archetype *is* indeed a thing and shapes how I help others. I was drawn to helping others because, in my younger years and as a child, I had received lots of praise and validation around being good and kind. I had learnt to be easy and pleasing and that my worth was in taking care of the emotional needs of others, and tuning out my own. This is what is often described as co-dependency in the literature.

When Will It Happen For Me

I'm quite sure that my attunement to the emotions of others was highly developed because of my Family of Origin Story. Our family of origin is simply the family we came from, and where we first come to understand love and relationships. Our family of origin story is made of the belief systems that have been instilled in us due to family conditioning. What about your family of origin? Consider themes such as conflict, expression or inhibition of emotions, mental health, sibling roles, gender roles, criticism, shame and neglect that have shaped who you are for better or worse. Within your story are big answers about why you do what you do. Here's a bit of my story, so it may help you shed light on your own.

From a young age, I developed a beautiful talent in noticing the emotions of others and comforting them. I was—and still am—hypersensitive and acutely aware of the shifting emotions of others. Like many women, this is a key piece of what I was taught about love. I thought love was taking care of another person, even functioning for them. How wrong I was. If you're a woman even a little bit like me, I want to help you undo this learning and conditioning, which much like brainwashing can be resistant to change. I want so much more for women. I want you to know and experience what love really is.

Love is so much more than what has been modelled to us, especially if we have experienced trauma and family dysfunction. And this is the sad reality; my urge to not be alone and longing to be truly loved was inextricably linked to my family of origin story. It propelled me down a path of failed relationships, because I went about enacting parts of that story; believing I needed to give more love in order to receive love, and if I did so, I wouldn't ever be lonely. Turns out a one-sided love is lonely. And the more we try to avoid our stories, especially in our search for love, the more they're going to impact us. The truth is, like most of us, I was at the whim of my past. I believe I was blindly led down this path due to my childhood conditioning, and what psychologists call trauma.

I understand trauma as an act of pain that forever shapes you. Trauma can be both big and small or more subtle. When I think about relationships and early life events in childhood, trauma often involves emotional or physical neglect, a lack of warmth or praise, a lack of emotional safety about sharing your feelings with a caregiver, and feeling dismissed and disconnected to your caregiver in important moments. It can involve not being seen or emotionally understood, or not being comforted and supported when you were feeling distress.

To put this in perspective, here's a bit of the narrative that I think shaped my future relationship trajectory for many years. I want you to meet my younger self, Little Phoebe. Unfortunately, Little Phoebe's parents fought, which included memories of screaming and shouting, which eventually resulted in them separating. Joining the pieces of my history together and deducting from my present self, it seems that Little Phoebe worried about her parents fighting, and the impact of this on her mum in particular. From memories that have been shared with me, Little Phoebe tried to nurture her mum, be there for her, and listen to her express her pain. I then progressed to spending a lot of my adult life trying to nurture, comfort and listen to others. This trait is both a beautiful gift and curse, that surely guided me to do the work that I do. I have both self-compassion and gratitude for this part of my inheritance. But I had to accept the painful reality of my relationship choices because of the stories and messages I had inherited about love.

More so, I suspect Little Phoebe missed her dad a lot after her parents' separation given what triggers me in my adult relationships

When Will It Happen For Me

(I found and still find emotional and physical distance from a partner truly triggering and anxiety-provoking, and it sends me into an anxious spin). It seems that Little Phoebe also worried about being left, and had the experience that her emotional needs weren't always met. So adult Phoebe had learnt that self-sacrificing and taking care of others needs kept relationship harmony and made her feel of value. And so, it is clear why recent adult Phoebe also chose partners with high emotional needs and went about nurturing and listening to them, at the expense of herself. We must join the dots of our past, imagine a timeline of defining relationship moments, and clarify how it plays out in the present. Doing so will set you free.

I tell you my story, because it represents the stories of many of the women I meet. It is the story of my female family members, clients, and friends of differing cultures and ages. They are stories of compromise, self-sacrifice, seeking the approval of others, and denying their own feelings, needs and desires in the service of the happiness of another. They are stories of suppressed voices, feeling misunderstood and unheard, and unsure if anyone cares about what they have to say. There are stories of keeping your deepest hurt and worry buried inside for fear of anger, confrontation, being dismissed, criticised or attacked. I've heard countless stories of females who feel powerless and scared to be honest and vulnerable for fear of being rejected or being told that they are too needy.

I'm thinking of one client, who was one of the most selfless women you could ever meet. I will never forget her because despite all of her hardships, she radiated warmth and immense gratitude for life. She joined the women's group to address her relationship patterns, and it soon dawned on her how much of her life had been dedicated to serving others—a legacy of being the most competent sibling in a large family and so she had quickly adopted a maternal role. When she announced to the group that this time in her life was going to be all about her and her self-care, I cheered for her. This woman's healing continued to blossom beautifully once she realised how much she had neglected her own needs and needed to make herself a priority.

We have each had a template of love imprinted upon us for better or worse, and when we can understand the template we were shown, we realise it is exactly that—a template, a story, and messaging, rather than the truth of how loveable and worthwhile you are. You have received conditioning passed on down through the generations that is rarely questioned or challenged. Your conditioning calls for updating.

Knowledge is Power

It is absolutely true that to understand love and the relationships we've chosen or ended up in, we have to go back in time and understand what our families taught us about love and relationships. My wording is deliberate because I think we can be too passive in our relationship choices. It is my hope that you cultivate deliberate intention throughout the course of your relationships, about who you choose to be with and the course your life takes. You can create the relationship you desire with intention.

Understanding my own upbringing in my family of origin has shed light on how and why I found myself in certain relationship dynamics. What my own parents modelled about relationships has no doubt had an impact on my own adult romantic relationships. Your own parents' relationship influences you, as the relationship of their parents influenced them. My hope is that for future generations, we develop greater insight and self-awareness, so that we can make intentional relationship choices, rather than be at the whim of our conditioning. Understanding is power.

This is how what we learn about love begins, our initial conditioning. Our caregivers are the ones who first model to us what love is. A mother may show her baby love through eye gaze, attentiveness to her baby's gestures for connection, and provides emotional warmth. The bond that is formed between an infant and her caregiver is what we call attachment, and this bond with our caregivers becomes our basis for how we connect with others, particularly with intimate romantic partners later in life.

If we are blessed with an emotionally available, present and attentive caregiver and have a calm temperament as an infant, we can be set up well for life and love. Unfortunately, some of us have received varying messages from our carers about our ability to seek comfort and be comforted by another, and have also received unclear messages about our worth and how deserving we are of love. And mostly, this is nobody's fault or intention. However, an absence of warmth, care and clear messages about how loveable we are leaves a legacy for us all.

I want you to deeply understand your attachment style and learnings. I want you to be deeply curious about your childhood, and reflect upon your learnings about the safety, reliability and security of others, and the imprint this has had on you. I want you to deeply know the narrative of your life and the events that shaped you, because it is only through knowing your background and trauma that you can re-create the narrative of your present life.

It is only through knowing what you emotionally missed out on that you can know what you need to give to yourself now, whether that be comfort, love or nurturing. Knowing what you inherited about love can bring about healing that starts with understanding and acceptance of your past, followed by compassion for yourself and others (carers, parents, guardians), and then finally giving back to yourself the pieces that were lacking (presence, empathy, a sense of worth, joy, play, healthy boundaries, and more). We will touch on the concept of being a parent to yourself and your inner child throughout the book because it is such a core piece of your healing. It was and remains the foundation of my healing.

So, ask yourself these questions now, with compassion and curiosity. Start with this:

- ♥ What did your parents or main caregivers show you about love?
- ♥ What messages did you receive from certain key persons and events about the meaning of love and relationships?
- ♥ What are your narratives about trust, dependability, independence, self-sufficiency, emotions, vulnerability, and worth?
- ♥ Consider, if there was conflict in your family, and if so, what did it mean to you?
- ♥ Did you receive warmth and affection, and the freedom to talk about your inner feelings, or were these elements missing?
- ♥ Were you told or shown that you mattered to someone?

And I'm not saying that we only inherited unfortunate legacies about our love and worth. Do look for the memories and moments that showed you that love is fair, reciprocal, and kind. Recall the moments that someone showed you that you were deeply worthy of love.

The truth is, a lot of us got mixed messages, and that can be confusing (on a side note, I often say it's no wonder love and finding a relationship is challenging given the differing messages that we have all received about how love should be. Putting two people together into a couple often requires a large degree of translating words and actions and clarifying meaning.) This stuff is painful to tap in to, but a vital part of our healing. I see these patterns and their impact every day in my practice, and as you can see via my own story, there is one big, bold realisation:

***We gravitate to what is familiar,
rather than what is good for us.***

Read that again.

At some point, I had to choose—and you do too. Do you gravitate to what is familiar, or what is good for you? I had to choose what parts of my inheritance to keep, and what parts to let go of. I decided to choose that I love my caring and nurturing heart, however it came to be part of me. I made a conscious choice to keep my open heart and emotional attunement, especially in my work. But—and this was a big but—I decided to change how much of my emotional energy I give to others, and to change how much I self-sacrifice. I had to deeply choose myself and to guard my energy. I would observe and listen to my energy levels when I am around different people, and I now deeply live by needing reciprocal relationships in my life. That is an absolute requirement for me, otherwise I opt out. If there is a balance of give and receive, expression of love, and fairness of the emotional, physical, mental and financial load, then my energy is safe and protected.

So, how do you want your relationships to feel? What will you choose to keep and let go of? This can define the health of your relationships for the rest of your life. The lessons are yours to own and take. You can throw out the old rules and rewrite the new ones. You get to redefine love at any stage. And that is truly empowering.

EXERCISE
Your Love Origin Story

To get even more clear on what you inherited from love and what patterns repeat in your romantic relationships, answer the following questions:

What did your family of origin teach you about relationships, for better or worse?

Rebuilding After a Breakup

What patterns do you need to be aware of in your own relationships?

If you struggle with partner choice and relationships, I want you to be able to clearly see your patterns and say to yourself: *"because of my past and what I was taught about love, I tend to choose partners that are (insert description). Whilst this type of partner feels familiar, I know it ultimately doesn't work for me. I will work to choose a partner who has qualities of (insert what you need to feel loved)."*

CHAPTER THREE

Rediscovering Your Old Self

As I look back on my last breakup, I will always remember the feeling of disbelief at what my life had become. It's a realisation I also see happening in my clients after a breakup, or during one.

You thought you knew who you were deeply inside and yet it feels like you're living a life miles apart from that person. You look at the apartment you're in—it's heavy, gloomy energy—and the toxic, unsalvageable shreds of a relationship around you, and it just doesn't resonate with the person you dreamt of being. You look at the person you are around your friends; the way you've pulled away from the people who matter to you to appease one person; the way you stop bringing up topics you feel passionate about, including mental health and social justice, for fear you will be talked over and shut down. You stop sharing your hobbies, interests, or achievements, in order to not shatter their fragile ego. You look at the hopes and dreams you had for the future for family and travel, and how you've abandoned them because they didn't fit your couples goals. Of course, compromise happens in the best relationships, but this is different—you've turned away from your sense of self.

I talked about grief in the previous chapter, and this is part of the equation; the heaviness of realising you can't keep going this way; the piercing feeling of knowing this is not the life you have set out to have, either alone or in a relationship. There is a great sadness in realising, you have stopped listening to your soul's wisdom. As the intensity of my destructive breakup and impending finale unfolded, I had repetitive moments of equal parts confusion and clarity. A lightning jolt that ran through my whole body, that woke me up and said, 'This is not you, this life is not who you are, and it is not what you stand for.'

I believe that we can only suppress our true selves for so long. On one level, I had great inner clarity because the voice inside of me felt so sure of who I was—my values, beliefs, ethics and dreams for my future. Yet I was confused because I was living in total misalignment with who I was. My bold voice was gone and my dreams were floating further off into the distance and that scared me. It was time to carve out my own path again towards a life of complete heart and soul alignment.

The Urge to Merge

My ex-partner and I moved into a shared apartment after only two or so months together, driven by what is often called an 'urge to merge'—a tendency to commit very quickly due to an intense emotional connection, often as a self-protection strategy. The merging of two individuals' lives offers reassurance and belonging for those with relationship insecurity.

As humans, we are programmed to pair off and procreate. We feel more protected in packs. In the heady days of early romance,

Rebuilding After a Breakup

we can become so intertwined with a person that we become one jigsaw that you make fit. My neural wiring led the way; I was primed to become attached and the anxious part of me felt safe in the hands of another. I can't blame my wiring; it was only doing what it thought was best. Looking back, however, I can see that my 'urge to merge' was superseding the red flags I was seeing.

The place we were going to live in was already a compromise; it didn't really meet my requirements, but it did work for my partner's needs. It felt more like a house than a home. He went about putting in fixtures that were not permitted, and little alarm bells started to ring inside me. Going against the rules of the rental property and making his own hinted at his entitlement. There were early signs of his lack of respect for my preferences. There had been earlier signs of his jealousy and 'love bombing' too, his irritability around my closeness to others. My pleasing and appeasing was there from the start. His insecurity and control was there from the start.

In a superbly short amount of time, my more authentic self, let's call her 'Old Phoebe', had been updated and replaced by 'Relationship Phoebe', who operated on one premise: do whatever it takes to keep the relationship. When we moved into the apartment, I thought that compromise would be the first of few. But, of course, it became the first of many. Looking back, it was a tried-and-tested pattern in my love life. I would begin a relationship feeling somewhat like myself and leave a relationship feeling like I didn't know who I was; by the end, Old Phoebe was dead and lost. She would shrink, and vanish, nowhere to be seen.

As I've shared, Relationship Phoebe is a version of me that begins to kick in when my relationships become rocky. It is a part of me that becomes blind to my relationship patterns, and operates on automatic pilot, at the whim of my conditioning. Relationship

When Will It Happen For Me

Phoebe was actually trying to be helpful, doing her best to help me find love. The problem was Relationship Phoebe was drawn to the love that I knew from my past, rather than the love that I needed in this life stage.

Because I was scared of losing love, believing I should take what I could get, I'd commit to a partner in a lightning flash, and then go along trying to discover the key to his happiness, rather than my own. And if the path got bumpy, perhaps because I had expressed a difference in opinion or idea, I'd quickly backtrack, apologise and suppress, to smooth the path over.

Relationship Phoebe would readily and automatically smooth over any relationship bumps at all costs, and Old Phoebe eventually vanished into thin air. Little sparks of her would creep through every now and then, thankfully. Eventually the sparks would ignite a fire in me but first I had to withstand a lot of heat and pressure.

Have you shrunk and become quieter, smaller, or less than, in the service of love? Who do you merge and morph into within your relationships? How much of yourself do you lose, and what parts have you held on to?

Within relationships, a lot of us subconsciously believe that if we give more love, we get more love in return. And at the whim of our subconscious conditioning, much like a leaf blowing in the breeze, you begin to get further away from your true nature. You see, underneath this conditioning, I believe we all have our true selves that are made up of our beliefs, likes, dislikes, values, interests, hobbies, talents, abilities, spirit. Our true selves are allowed to exist when they receive unconditional love, and our true selves thrive and shine through in the presence of nurturing, accepting others. Our true self feels lighter, brighter, relaxed,

Rebuilding After a Breakup

playful, enthusiastic, connected to life. The expression of our true self feels more joyful and open, rather than repressed and suppressed. A lot of my clients hide parts of their true self for fear of conflict, rejection, abandonment, or being shamed by another. Initially hiding your true self feels easier, and eventually it feels heavy, builds resentment, and restricts you from receiving love. There is such freedom when you are your true self. Somewhere along the way, and often across several relationships, we become less of our true selves and some unrecognisable version of self. There was never anything wrong with your true nature, the issue lies in the conditioning you received.

I have met countless women who equally appear to suffer from losing themselves, getting quickly absorbed into relationships and becoming whoever they need to be in order to keep the connection and ensure their partner's happiness. And this process just happens, often without awareness, as a slow descent, and then one day you wake up angry and not recognising yourself anymore.

I once had a client who was so devastatingly in love with her partner, whom could be described as moody, defensive and unpredictable. My client did everything in her power to soothe him: over-apologise, accept his moodiness and distance, question her own version of reality, accept faults for all their disagreements, and stop seeing certain friends that triggered him. Over many sessions I had to remind her how a healthy relationship looks and feels, as she was clearly over-functioning in this dynamic. I saw my role as reminding her of her worth and capacity to receive love, being enough as she was.

Sit in the reality of what can happen to women in relationships, and ask yourself when you have been your most true self. It may alarm you, and if it does, that's okay. You're in the right place.

If you've reading this, and it resonates with you, I want to give you some hope for reconciliation. As I've discovered, it is possible to re-find yourself again. You always have a choice to rediscover and reignite your old self, and you can break the pattern of self-abandonment in relationships.

If you're going through a breakup, or considering leaving a relationship, it can be the perfect fuel for finding yourself. Doing something brave and ballsy, like leaving a dead-end relationship, job or past does something to you. You leave and emerge with a new lens on life, and with fierce determination to live life on your own terms, perhaps for the first time ever. Never to look back again and totally reclaim yourself.

Of course, it doesn't happen by chance—you need to do the work to make it happen. After my final breakup in that August of 2021, I went on a mission to bring back Old Phoebe. Old Phoebe was who I needed to find and rediscover. Old Phoebe has the most beautiful qualities and foundations, and I really needed to get back to her, because in Old Phoebe my happiness lay. Did I do it? Well, she's the one writing this book—and, when she came back, she came back with bells on! Read how ...

How To Re-Find Yourself

If you are anything like me, you too may have lost yourself within a relationship. If you have tended to pair up with insecure or emotionally needy partners, you may have suppressed core parts of your identity in order to please and pacify a difficult partner whose emotional needs seemed to outweigh your own. If you know the pain and regret of losing yourself, my heart goes out to you. Let's

Rebuilding After a Breakup

make sure this never happens again. I hope my story of rebirth gives you both validation and inspiration. You can rebirth yourself at any point along your journey. This is your life story to create.

There is, and can be, so much beauty after the end of a relationship because it offers time and space to be alone; to be with you and reconnect with lost parts of yourself. In the solitude and quiet of being alone again, you can (re)figure out who you really are. You can get back to 'old you'—your most raw, authentic and real self. One of my clients spoke about how she had always loved visiting museums and outdoor markets, but gave all those things away quite early on in her relationship. After her breakup, we spoke about her getting back into museums, theatre and reconnecting with old friends. It was a pleasure to witness her bring joy back into her life. The loss of herself was perhaps the very lesson she needed.

After being frustrated with conceding to and giving to another, and being emotionally drained, you can connect with you again. You can feel the pressure melt away. You may also go through waves of confusion, shame and disappointment, and grieve having lost touch with the things that make you thrive. You may need to shed old memories or old belongings in the home that remind you of what you had become or had stopped being. And as you shed these layers, may you emerge like a butterfly from her cocoon, slowly and gently at first, and then liberated as you are welcomed back to life on your terms.

You may be sitting with a deep knowing of who you are or may need some help discovering and rebuilding parts of you.

If it is the latter, here are my suggestions:

- ♥ Start with getting clear on your unique strengths and qualities. How do those trusted others in your inner circle see you? Think of the ones that allow your light to shine the brightest, that have known you across time and have received the gift of your presence. The ones who saw through your relationship mask and know the real you.

- ♥ What are you good at in life? Consider your talents at work, with creativity, with people, and at home.
- ♥ What was your younger self always talented in and capable of? Consider the interests and hobbies you have always had, dating as far back as childhood, that bring you a sense of joy and fulfilment, and get to participating in those.
- ♥ What is your true personality? Are you more extroverted and get energy from being around others, or are you more introverted and prefer deeper one on one conversations or being lost in your own internal world? Are you an emotional, heart-centred soul who needs to get back in touch with her feelings and longings, or a more rational and logical thinker that is a seeker of knowledge, information and facts?
- ♥ What do you value most in life, and what brings your life meaning? Write down some personal goals that are aligned with your values, and get to work.

Whoever you are, it is important you nourish all these aspects of yourself that may have been buried for some time. The burying of parts of ourselves has likely pre-dated your romantic relationships. For example, maybe you were told that your love of dancing and play was frivolous and silly, and life is all about study, hard work and earning money to get ahead. Don't be afraid to get in touch with your inner child and play, explore, draw, go on adventures, and get lost in the moment of a new experience. And if you

Rebuilding After a Breakup

need to share your story and the breakdown of your relationship and loss of self, do that.

Surround yourself with your tribe; the ones who see you for who you are, and make you feel loved. If you had suppressed emotions to survive, you are now safe to be vulnerable, and know that this sensitive part of you is of worth. It is the part of you that allows you to connect with others. Use your singlehood to deliberately and intentionally discover and define who you are. If you listen to the wisdom of your emotions, body and heart, they will show you the way.

During these times of feeling my feelings, my own personal rebirth, I adopted my beautiful toy Cavoodle puppy, Bella. She got me in touch with my nurturing and playful nature, and helped me prioritise what really matters: our time together. I could develop boundaries around our needs. I deeply needed to receive love and care more than ever, and Bella provided that. Receiving love as women is our nature. I also found self-expression in music and language, and went out of my way to connect with a tribe of like-minded single women who could empathise with the realities of my current struggle. And I threw myself into my work, which gave me a sense of competency and has always been purposeful. There is nothing more valuable to me than helping others heal. All of these things helped me feel like me again.

I truly believe that there are times in life when being selfish is necessary, and rediscovering yourself after a breakup, or at any point in your relationship, is one of them. I don't mean selfish in a cold way either. I simply mean allowing space and time to focus on you, giving yourself permission to say 'no' to what doesn't serve you, and filling your own cup first. This will put you in a better position for your relationships. Once you have nurtured yourself first and have restored your own energy, you are more able to connect with others.

Being your most true self creates space for the right people to come in to your life, and filters out the ones who will end up causing you hurt and pain. You truly deserve to live life on your own terms, after all you've been through. And I'm pretty sure you'll love the old you. Filling the spaces in your life with things that fulfill you will ensure you are less at risk of giving these things up in future relationships.

One final note: you may wish to update the old you several times over—after all, life changes us. Whilst I loved having my old self back, complete with honesty, integrity, playfulness and softness, this final breakup had changed me and additional qualities of more self-belief, firmer boundaries, and an attitude of 'I deserve and am worthy' were added in the mix. This was who I was meant to be. I wish you this sense of assuredness, clarity, determination and spirit too.

EXERCISE
How to Come Alive Inside

Take a few moments to think about or journal the following questions:

What parts of you did you lose, if any, in this relationship? Write the parts of you that you would like to rediscover here.

What are the qualities, strengths and traits that you want to further add in?

When Will It Happen For Me

When do I feel most energised and alive?

If one sentence or word jumps out at you, which describes your most alive self, it can be helpful to write it on a Post-It note and stick it somewhere where you'll glance at it regularly (your mirror, by your kettle, in your car). Sometimes, we need a reminder to come back to ourselves until it feels natural again.

CHAPTER FOUR
The Upside of Anger

Tidal waves of rage hit me when I called off my relationship that August. I remember getting angry, really angry. I knew this was good. I knew it was good because, in previous breakups, instead of being angry, I'd fall into a horrible depression and was paralysed by fear. I'd then self-blame and self-shame, questioning what was my fault, and what could I have done to be worthy of his love. Not this time. This time I was radically justified in my anger, more sure of myself and the love I deserved.

To me, it was a sign that my self-respect was intact; that I knew I needed more from a relationship, and that I was prepared to stand up for myself. As women, we can label anger as a shameful and ugly emotion. Anger, however, is a useful force for a woman if tapped into and expressed in the right way, and this is what I always tell my clients.

I was angry about how I had been treated, the lack of fairness and reciprocity in my final imbalanced relationship. In the last chapter, I discussed my in-built 'urge to merge' and my tendency to lose myself in a relationship, however, it was never just one-sided. In order to lose yourself, you usually need to be with a person who is willing for you to do it. In my partner's case, he was extremely intense in his opinions, unwilling to compromise and extremely happy for my desires to be overshadowed. He was also complicit in me carrying more of the economic load whilst he sorted out his career, and criticised my mood after challenging days at work. I felt no choice but to hide medical appointments out of fear of his anger, as he did not agree with how I chose to take care of my health. He was strongly against the Covid vaccine, and I had grown up in a family of health professionals. I struggle to write a lot of this now as it crystalises the abuse I experienced, and how trapped I felt. It makes it all real.

I didn't want to see it until I had to face it—when the relationship was over. That's when the anger flooded in and speeded up in intensity. Some people might say you have to let go of anger. Of course, as a clinician, I agree they are right. Anger is toxic when we cling onto it and store it in our bodies, but it can be an incredibly powerful signpost when we look at what it's telling us. And, when we listen to it, it's usually easier to release it.

Anger is a gift, a fast, undeniable emotion that needs to be looked at. It was the emotion that helped me get back on the right life path. In my case, after my breakup, I knew what my boundaries were more than ever, and that I deserved respect, fairness, nurturing and warmth. I also deserved a partner who filled himself up rather than depending on me to do that for him.

Consider your own relationship with anger and your beliefs about this emotion. Do you allow yourself to feel it? Is it acceptable to you? Women are often shamed for their anger and self-expression, and I believe that narrative is outdated and needs to be updated.

Sometimes in life you go through something so profound, so earth-shatteringly transformative, that your approach to life will never be the same again. That breakup started a revolution within me. A revolution of change and a new approach to life, love, and relationships. There was a powerful, undeniably angry and fierce force within me; a loud voice that said you are going to find your way through this.

It said to me, 'You are going to make sure you never, ever go through something like this again. You're not going to spend any more of your precious life in relationships that drain you and destroy you.'

I will forever be thankful, not ashamed, of the anger I felt in that moment, and the lesson it taught me; a lesson which has gone on to revolutionise my life.

Rage Is A Roadmap

Have you ever made a vow to yourself to fundamentally change the way you do relationships? Perhaps you should. A promise, a vow, a commitment to truly understand and unpack your baggage; to own it, be accountable, and decide to not let it define you for the rest of your life. This is the path down which I was headed. And, if you start to notice anger, frustration, or burning slowly inside you, I suggest you get curious about it. What is your dear friend, anger, communicating to you? If you're feeling a sense of rage, can it provide you with a roadmap—a clear set of directions for how to move forward with clearer boundaries and clarity?

I had experienced heartbreak before, and I had experienced a loss of self within my relationships before, but this time it was different. I had never gotten to the end of a relationship and felt so unlike myself; so out of touch with the essence of my being. And that was equally terrifying and confronting.

For me, my anger led me deep into therapy, which is probably not surprising for a therapist (I do try to practise what I preach, sometimes!). I had started back in therapy some months before the end of the relationship, desperate for support navigating my experience, and to unpack whether this relationship had any healthy elements or was indeed a lost cause. You think I'd be able to answer that question myself, however, we do get lost inside our own emotional world and lose rationality, and cling on to hope to avoid the pain ahead.

I spent many sessions with my own psychologist discussing my ex—his trauma and his anger—and unconsciously denying and minimising my own feelings. My assertively skilled therapist kept me on track. He worked relentlessly to get me in touch with my emotions. I really wasn't enjoying the aftermath of these sessions, which left me feeling tired, depleted, and overwhelmingly depressed.

Sometimes, I'd spend the whole day back in bed after a therapy session feeling totally incapable of doing anything else, all my energy drained from my body. I wanted to quit the sessions, but I didn't. I knew what I'd tell my own clients: try to trust the process of feeling the pain and know that you are, gradually, rebuilding yourself. I'd remind them that they are strong enough to sit with all those feelings.

I was particularly angry about his lack of responsibility and accountability at the end. He left me with considerable half-paid wedding bills to negotiate, and refused to engage in reasonable conversations about the best path forward. I was so angry about my financial disadvantage because of who and what I had allowed in my life. However, I was incredibly angry that rather than talk to me face-to-face, a family member called me only days after he left, to ask for my engagement ring back. That made me rage inside and out. Not about the ring itself, but the fact that their priorities were financial, rather than having genuine interest for my wellbeing.

I have tried several techniques to manage my anger post-breakup, and here's what has helped the most. When I went to the gym, I would imagine the offender (my ex) in my mind, and let loose in a boxing class. It allowed me to channel this feeling in a healthy way, without causing damage. What I also did was redecorate the apartment and purge the space of any of his belongings as soon as possible. This helped me redefine the space as my own and symbolised doing life on my own terms again. And I would turn to my journal, and express the anger I was feeling, which was a way to validate and allow my emotions. And in therapy, I simply needed to vent and express myself, and benefitted from being reassured that how I was being treated was unacceptable.

Cooling The Heat

If you are getting caught in an ongoing trap of entitled and justified anger, ask yourself if it is really helping you heal. I had to acknowledge that my anger towards him was only helpful to a point—it could help me define new boundaries and a life direction, but it wasn't going to change what he had done or would do going forward. He wasn't going to become a more evolved human being because of my angry self-expression. In fact, our anger never changes anyone nor does it cause them to take us seriously (it has quite the opposite effect!) Our anger is for us only, it is ours to soothe and settle alone.

I am reminded of one woman I worked with several years ago in couples therapy. She was understandably angry as she carried the bulk of the financial, emotional and parental load of the family, and her husband just wasn't pulling his weight. My role was to both validate her anger, but equally show her that it was going to do further damage to her relationship, rather than get her needs met. She had to learn to walk away, breathe, validate her own anger, and then more directly communicate her needs, rather than give up on expressing herself altogether.

If anger is acknowledged, expressed and then released in a healthy way, it slowly subsides. When anger is heard and validated, it softens, and then space is made for the more vulnerable emotions underneath to be revealed. Emotions such as grief, hurt, and fear can then be felt. In fact, whenever I meet an angry client I'm not overly focused on or concerned about their anger. I simply set about asking questions about what's happening more deeply inside for them, attempting to bypass the anger and connect with their hurt. Anger is most often a smoke screen disguising something more painful.

So, what eases the hot, burning flames of anger? Start with validation, recognition, and compassion. I was able to let go of anger in bursts by having empathy for my own story, and sitting with my sadness and anxiety more. Instead of beating myself up for the situation, I'd remind myself of the events in my life story that led me to this point, and that took away some of the self-blame.

If you are in a relationship and anger and resentment is burning for you, see if you can find empathy for your partner, like one of my clients did. We had worked hard to identify her

Rebuilding After a Breakup

cycle of conflict in her relationship, and it was sinking in. Rather than attacking or blaming her partner, or assuming his behaviour was ill-intentioned, she was able to self-regulate, breathe, and remain curious about his experiences, which resulted in new understanding and compassion for her partner. She was able to appreciate the stress and burdens on him in a new way, and her anger cooled down.

If you are struggling to detach from your anger, you need to find your self-discipline. Your firm voice that reminds you of the futility of your anger and encourages you to stay on course. As often as you must, imagine breathing out all of your anger, and sending it away. You must also actively choose to embrace a spirit of gratitude for your life lessons. See if you can deliberately cultivate more gratitude and focus on what life gives you (freedom, nature, sunshine), rather than what it doesn't (a relationship for example). Freedom, joy, and gratitude are vibrant emotions which oppose anger. It is hard to feel angry when you can appreciate life and its bountiful gifts. This practice may not come naturally to you, and that is okay. However, in order to restore happiness, you must choose to notice the good. I chose to focus on my freedom and the excitement of an unwritten future. You can start smaller—a whole bed to yourself, a cleaner living space, an undisturbed morning coffee, or the morning song of the birds in spring.

And if anger pops up every now and again (I'm quite sure it will, based on my own journey) start by validating it and soothing it via breathing, creative expression, or intentionally choosing to let it go. How did I not rage when I was reminded of my ex? For a while I did rage and couldn't wish him well. My anger wanted him to suffer. Too honest? And now I realise his suffering won't change my life, only I can do that. I choose to take the good from this experience, and whilst I struggle to be grateful to him, I am honestly grateful to life and the profoundly challenging experiences I've had that have shaped me. I hope one day, your anger also melts, and the space for joy and gratitude, freedom and newness grows and grows.

EXERCISE
Don't Supress, Do Express Your Anger

Take a few moments to think about and complete the following:

Validate your anger. Write what you are angry about, and why this anger is valid.

_____
_____
_____
_____

Anger is your teacher. Write what your anger has taught you about your needs and boundaries, as well as what you deserve.

_____
_____
_____
_____

How may you express your anger so that it moves out of you? Consider journaling, creativity or exercise.

_____
_____
_____
_____

When Will It Happen For Me

Note the more vulnerable emotions that lay under your anger.

If you notice your anger becoming too rigid or persistent, write how you can soothe it. Write why cooling your anger is helpful.

Think about what you are grateful for that softens your anger.

PART TWO

Repatterning For Love

CHAPTER FIVE
Healing Your Wounds

A month or so had passed after my breakup; my emotions had settled some more, and out of the blue came a realisation that I needed to have a stern conversation with myself. It was a typical day at home, alone in the apartment, and the heavy clouds of sorrow that had been encroaching upon me lifted and were replaced by determination.

I needed to face myself with courage and speak the disappointing truth. It's as if I took myself warmly yet firmly by the hand, sat myself down and we had a serious talk. I looked at myself in the eye with compassion and clarity, and said, 'I love you but enough of this pattern. I know you'd like to think that you know how to have healthy relationships by now, but this just isn't true.'

In that moment, I made a vow to myself to stop dating the same version of a partner, and to stop placing myself in the same unhealthy relationship cycle. I remember saying to myself, out loud, 'It is time you vowed to yourself to never do that again. It's time to figure this all out once and for all.'

And I internally agreed, 'Okay. Show me the way.'

So, I got out my trusty, shiny laptop with access to all the possible information about love and healthy relationships and went searching. I started my search with relationship coaches, curiously and instinctively hoping that they could help me on my mission. In my gut, no one really resonated for me; many so-called dating gurus felt phony and salesy, and seemed to offer outcomes that were just too good to be true.

I remember asking a group of colleagues their thoughts on dating coaches and they all relayed stories of clients who had been given false promises, given away thousands of dollars, and been left adrift and without love. So, I turned back to psychology, the field that has provided me a much-loved career and a solid base of knowledge.

I was stubborn and relentless in my search, ever dedicated to my quest of searching for love. For years, I would feel ashamed of my quest for love and felt shamed by those who told me to be happy on my own. Please don't buy into that narrative—to have love and desire love is a basic human need. And one day during my quest, through the screen of my computer, I came across the very thing I needed—Schema Therapy. At that point in time, I didn't realise how monumental that moment would be for me. In fact, it was so pivotal to my journey that, over the next two chapters, I'll share more about Schema Therapy and how it's shaped me, my work, and how I met my current partner (spoiler alert!).

Schema Therapy 101

Schema Therapy is a model of psychological therapy founded by Psychologist Jeff Young, originating in 1990. Of all the models of

Repatterning For Love

therapy I have studied, I like this one the most. It tells the story of our humanity and conditioning. When I introduce clients to this way of working; they experience such relief and validation. They feel Schema Therapy tells the story of their lives, loves, losses.

Schema Therapy focuses on the relationship patterns and learnings we inherit from childhood experiences and trauma. From the start of this book, I have wanted to emphasise the power of these early life influences upon us. Due to early life events in childhood and the influences of parenting, we inherit ways of seeing the world. The ways in which we see the world are called schemas. Schemas are comprised of cognitions, emotions, bodily sensations, and patterns of behaviour.

More broadly, schemas are pervasive belief systems and patterns that show up in our lives repetitively, and secretly drive our behaviour. The theory is, our schemas or unhelpful belief systems can lead to low self-esteem, lack of connection to others, problems expressing emotions, and even excessive worrying about basic safety issues. These beliefs can even contribute to strong attraction to inappropriate partners, lead to dissatisfying careers, and keep us stuck and unfulfilled in life.

I had studied Schema Therapy in more recent years but had never seen this modality applied to finding love. In fact, I hadn't come across any clear examples in my own field of psychologists helping clients find love. And why not? Given that love is such a basic human need, to me, it felt very relevant. And, so, I became a dedicated student of Schema Therapy.

When I began exploring Schema Therapy in relation to love and romance, I turned to my colleague and mentor, Dr Tracey Hunter, a Clinical Psychologist and Schema Therapist, who translated this work into real-life, practical skills that equipped me for dating and navigating love. For her wisdom and guidance, I am incredibly grateful. This work felt revolutionary and important.

One of my strengths is that I am a seeker of knowledge. I also enjoy being a student of life. I always believed that there were answers to my very serious relationship questions. In those moments, it became glaringly obvious: if I truly addressed my core wounds from childhood and beyond, I would develop a healthier relationship with myself, which would set me up for a healthier romantic relationship.

And so, from that day forward, I took Tracey's wisdom and advice very seriously, and within a few months my life was transformed. I want to acknowledge that what has made me a better therapist and healer is working through my own stuff. I have walked the walk, and know what it takes to heal. This period of intense self-work using approaches from Schema Therapy, gave me a template for healing and a clear roadmap for finding a loving relationship. So, let me show you what I learnt.

The Power of Our Patterns

It is true that our foundational years in life imprint upon us and can guide behaviour for the rest of our lives. When I began to explore Schema Therapy in relation to my relationships and my family of origin story, as told through the lens of schemas, everything crystalised. Once I could identify my own personal schemas or worldviews (of which there are currently eighteen, which I outline below), I could begin to observe and label my thoughts and feelings, and identify the behaviours that were clearly driving my relationship disasters.

Repatterning For Love

In Schema Therapy, beginning with a series of assessments, people learn to recognise which schemas and problematic coping styles (called 'modes' in Schema Therapy) affect them the most. With Schema Therapy, you come to truly understand the origins of your behaviour and learn how to make lasting changes.

There are eighteen core schemas or worldviews that are thought to impact us and drive behaviour, and research is currently exploring the possibility of additional schemas existing. Let me share these schemas with you now, and see if any of these feelings resonate with you.

The Eighteen Core Schemas are:

- ♥ **Fear of Abandonment / Instability:** you feel a lot of anxiety in relationships, or tend to avoid them altogether due to a fear that you will ultimately be left.
- ♥ **Mistrust / Abuse:** you have difficulty trusting others and fear that ultimately others can't be trusted.
- ♥ **Emotional Deprivation:** you feel no one has truly been there for you to nurture you nor understand your emotional world.
- ♥ **Defectiveness / Shame:** you tend to feel not good enough inside and doubt your worth and lovability.
- ♥ **Social Isolation / Alienation:** you tend to feel different to others and a bit of a loner.
- ♥ **Dependence / Incompetence:** you worry that you are incapable of coping with life on your own.
- ♥ **Vulnerability to Harm or Illness:** you often worry about something bad happening.
- ♥ **Enmeshment / Undeveloped Self:** you tend to adopt the views of others, particularly family, to the point you don't know who you are.

- ♥ **Failure to Achieve:** you feel like a failure in your life, and that you have not achieved.
- ♥ **Entitlement / Grandiosity:** you feel that you are better than and above others.
- ♥ **Insufficient Self-Control / Self-Discipline:** you tend to struggle to regulate your emotions and execute important tasks.
- ♥ **Subjugation:** you struggle to be assertive and fear confrontation, including another's anger, or being controlled.
- ♥ **Self-Sacrifice:** you feel that the needs of others are more important than your own.
- ♥ **Approval-Seeking / Recognition-Seeking:** you highly value what others think of you, you like to be liked, and your worth is based heavily on the opinion of others.
- ♥ **Negativity / Pessimism:** you tend to have a negative outlook on life and struggle to be optimistic.
- ♥ **Emotional inhibition:** you are uncomfortable with emotions and view them as a sign of weakness, or they cause you embarrassment.
- ♥ **Unrelenting Standards / Hyper-Criticalness:** you set incredibly high standards and are perfectionistic.
- ♥ **Punitiveness:** you believe that punishment is warranted towards yourself and/ or others when mistakes are made.

Some of these schemas tend to present more commonly in my female clients, particularly those in my women's group. In particular, I have observed higher levels of fear of abandonment, defectiveness, emotional deprivation, self-sacrifice, approval-seeking, subjugation, and unrelenting standards, amongst my

Repatterning For Love

female clients who are longing for a healthier love. I think this says incredible amounts about our conditioning and how we've learnt to get our needs for love met.

Personally, I struggled largely with emotional deprivation, fear of abandonment, and shame. I wonder what is speaking to you from the list. You may equally read the list, and it will shed light on past partners and their own core wounds that were triggered within your relationship.

So, how does this apply to love, you ask? Picture this. Let's say your parents separated, or one parent was emotionally unavailable, and you were a sensitive young person and tended to worry. This may have contributed to the development of an underlying Fear of Abandonment Schema.

These early life experiences may have caused you anxiety about the reliability and presence of critical others, and so as a coping mechanism you may have become hypervigilant to signs of emotional disconnection. This hypervigilance facilitated your survival; however, it also became your relationship template. And as an adult, you may have been drawn to partners who created this familiar feeling of anxiety within you.

Or, as can unfortunately be the case, your anxiety or hypervigilance may overwhelm a partner who doesn't know how to respond. This can result in actual abandonment if your partner struggles to be responsive to your anxiety. They are exhausted from trying to soothe and reassure or they pull away, and you end up feeling alone. This reminds me of one of my clients who was justifiably terrified when she started dating a healthy male partner. She carried the wounds of past relationships with her, fearing that her new partner would withdraw from her and eventually leave, as her ex-partner had done. In order to manage this fear of abandonment, she kept her worries to herself and struggled to communicate her needs to her new partner. Her failure to open up nearly sabotaged the relationship. Fortunately, with my urging she opened up just in time. She was met with a tad of frustration and disappointment, but ultimately a greater level of closeness than she had ever experienced. This was the first relationship she felt truly safe to be herself in. Later on, I'll unpack more about how to soothe yourself when this anxiety kicks in.

See how our schemas can lead us down unhelpful paths and set us up for relationship mishaps and errors, particularly when we are blinded to the forces at play because no one has ever told you this.

What did my initial exploration of Schema Therapy show me? That I had to take four steps. I had to:

- ♥ Know my schemas
- ♥ Own my relationship history, particularly the failures
- ♥ Assess my relationship fears and sense of worth; and
- ♥ Observe my life from a bird's-eye view in real time and deeply question each feeling, thought and trigger, especially on the road ahead into dating and potential relationships.

Here's how my new approach looked as I embarked on this next chapter of my life. Quickly and early on, I had to begin to look out for relationships that were emotionally unsafe, and be more intentional in co-creating emotionally safe relationships based on vulnerable communication. I had to learn how to soothe myself when my schemas or wounds were triggered, and I had to learn the difference between unhealthy relationships that reinforced my

Repatterning For Love

schemas, versus healthy relationships that triggered my schemas and signalled that I had work to do.

Some partners we attract are truly toxic, as is their behaviour, so of course, we'd be triggered. And other partners unintentionally trigger us, often because our own triggers are so super sensitive. We have felt anxious and guarded and our own alarm bells go off too quickly, even in the face of safety. This is the tricky part—all relationships will ultimately trigger our wounds, even the most loving ones. The hallmark of a loving relationship is being responsive and loving in the face of each other's triggers.

In the next chapter, we'll explore the next step in Schema Therapy—how to explore core skills that heal negative patterns. For now, let's do an exercise to begin to explore your schemas (please do this with a therapist if it helps you to feel supported). What patterns in your early life can be linked to your current relationship behaviours? Be curious, be compassionate, and see what it brings up for you.

EXERCISE
What's Your Worldview?

Take a few moments to think about and complete the following:

Look again at the schemas from the list above (see pages 65–66). Write three here that resonate most for you.

List the emotions that arise for you, looking at the schemas you've chosen.

Repatterning For Love

Which of these schemas do you feel most drawn to shift, and why?

CHAPTER SIX
Core Skills That Heal

After some time in therapy, and with a new found understanding of my schemas, I felt like I wanted to date again. My biology—my 'urge to merge' feelings and longing for connection—had wanted to date months before I actually did start to date. If it was up to my biology, I likely would have started sooner but the wisdom of therapy told me to slow down.

In reality, I started my first steps towards dating only four months after my breakup. It was close to Christmas time. I've always felt that this time of year is one of hope, complete with warm summer evenings, emerging new year's resolutions and the possibility of dreams coming true; a time when the city felt more energised and alive, and celebrations were to be had.

The whirlpool of emotions inside of me had also started to ease and subside. I felt a little less melancholy and more engaged with life. I wanted love in my life again—a different type of love; one that would take me as I am, my true self. A love that would offer an encouraging base of support and reliability. Some would say it was too soon, and I hear you. I had been through a lot.

I had called off a wedding, promptly adopted a puppy and had my eggs frozen. Oh, I forgot to mention this part earlier! Sometime after my breakup, one of my most supportive and wise friends reminded me that my biological clock was ticking, and it may be wise to take action. And so I did. For now, all I'll share is it was one of the more emotional experiences of my life. Perhaps, that's a story for another time.

Let's get back to dating: Was the timing right? Was I crazy to be considering dating again? Perhaps! I still don't really know the answer to that. But what I do know is that dating facilitated my healing.

Female clients often pose the question, 'when is the right time to date after a breakup?' What I generally tell them is, whilst I don't think there are any firm timeframes, you must ask yourself if you have enough strength and internal resources to ride the bumps of dating.

Of course, I didn't take my own advice. I dived into dating before being truly resourceful enough to do so (okay, I don't really recommend it but it worked out for me). Because I cultivated those skills and that resilience whilst I was dating, rather than truly having a multitude of coping resources before I started. I'm not necessarily saying do what I did but, if you must, do it with the support and guidance of someone you trust, such as a therapist.

I had spent a lot of time grieving, reflecting, wondering, pondering, reading self-help books on dating and relationships, and my energy was different. With the support of my trusted therapist and newly discovered Schema Therapy tools, I decided to dip my toe back into the dating pool with Schema Therapy serving as my floatation device for navigating challenging currents.

Embodying A Healed You

Knowing your schemas and wounds provides a lot of insight and validation. Prior to my women's healthy relationships group that I run as part of my practice, I have each woman complete a schema questionnaire. I score it up for them and give feedback of the results, including suggesting areas for growth.

I remember opening one woman's email reply that said, 'that's so me, it really speaks to who I am in relationships', regarding her approval-seeking nature and challenges with assertiveness due to fear of confrontation. Other women have felt sad and confronted as they realise their schemas and must grieve for their younger selves.

I know how it feels. When I first learnt about my schemas, I felt validated when emotional deprivation and fear of abandonment were exposed in therapy. This spoke to my experience of feeling I had missed some nurturing and emotional attunement in early life. However, when these schemas began to heal a bit, they lifted and exposed a defectiveness schema. I ultimately felt shame about my own emotions and had deep longing for the soothing of others. I had always felt my emotions made me needy and couldn't be accepted by others. When I could finally feel the shame sitting in my body, the grief for my younger self cascaded out of me. I was simultaneously sad and shocked that I had shamed myself.

Despite the pain of this work, I knew that doing this self-exploration would be worth it. The work really begins when women begin to embody the opposite of their schemas. In order to truly heal, we must target three schema components: thoughts or beliefs, emotions and memories, and behaviours.

Thoughts and beliefs:

The unhelpful and rigid beliefs of your schemas must be addressed. This involves actively shifting the beliefs that have been holding you back, challenging these beliefs and looking for exceptions to these unkind, often irrational beliefs to develop a more reasonable and loving self-narrative. For me this involved challenging the belief that my emotions were too much. I practiced reminding myself that my sensitivity and emotions were a relational gift and quality that would be appreciated by the right partner. Instead of believing that my emotions were weak, I began to see them as a strength that helped me connect to others. I reminded myself over and over that my emotions were valid, welcome, and made me human. They were nothing to be ashamed of and deserved to be heard and shared. I also had to challenge the belief that I would be alone forever, and realise that just wasn't likely (especially if I applied myself to dating). That I was a beautiful person who would meet her person in time.

To shift any unhelpful and hurtful beliefs associated with the schema, I would ask myself:

Where did I learn this belief from?
What tells me that this belief isn't true?
What is a more realistic and compassionate belief about me?

Emotions and memories:

To rebalance your belief system, it's important to welcome in emotions that oppose your schemas. For example, if you have a fear-based schema, such as vulnerability to harm, subjugation, or fear of abandonment, you may experience large amounts of anxiety. You may have memories that you link with emotions of anxiety, worry, and fear.

Repatterning For Love

In order to heal, your mind, heart, and body must learn to experience peace, calm, and stability—and to trust it. This can be done through a variety of practices including relaxation, meditation, and my favourite—imagery. Through imagery, it is possible to connect with more trust, joy, confidence, hope, and optimism.

For me, this involved imagining myself with my future partner. I would be relaxed and carefree in his company, because he was taking care of organising the day. I had always longed for a partner who embodied a team spirit, and so I visualised feeling that in his presence. When I was dating and fearing abandonment, I would go for walks with my puppy and imagine holding my inner child by the other hand. I had a family already and was connected and cared for. Stay tuned for more on inner child work.

Behaviours:

In order to heal, you must consciously and deliberately minimise behaviours that reinforce your schema. For example, if you have a failure schema, you may procrastinate and avoid taking risks, which exaggerates this schema. Or, if you have a mistrust schema, you may avoid dating altogether, and in doing so, sabotage yourself meeting kind others, who could help you shift this belief.

Learning to develop skills in judgment and discernment can only be developed by engaging in the world. To overcome a mistrust schema, you must remember that trust is built upon the gradual and reciprocal exchange of vulnerable disclosures. For me, this involved acting as if I was comfortable with my own emotions and vulnerable parts. This work tapped into my emotional deprivation schema in particular and involved validating my own emotions. Being more accepting of my own emotions facilitated me sharing these with others. When I started dating my partner, I worked on sharing my relationship needs and my emotional experience of him being disconnected. This ultimately helped us connect more. Similarly, with my fear of abandonment schema, I had to learn to sit with normal distance when dating, rather than pursuing and frantically texting. This behaviour facilitated the growth of more reciprocal connections, and allowed me to ultimately end up with a non-abandoning partner who chose to reach out to me. These steps allowed me to be myself and also helped the defectiveness schema shrink.

At the end of this chapter, I'll share my Go-To Core Skills For Healing—the practical methods, that helped to shift all of the above.

Your Most Important Relationship

Now, I know this is something you've likely heard before, but the relationship that you have with yourself is the most important one that you will ever have. As a therapist, of course I knew this, but it became very apparent and unavoidable when I dipped my toe back into the dating pool.

Your relationship with yourself has the most potential to offer you stability, security, safety, love, presence and connection. Your relationship with yourself will also predict the quality of your relationships with others. How do I know this? I have lived it, and I witness it in my therapy room each and every day of practice. Clients who present with more self-love and compassion are less triggered by the emotional world of their partner and their relationship because they are more sure of who they are and do not personalise the feedback of their partner. Their self-worth allows them to have a more balanced and rational perspective of themselves and their partner.

A healthy connection to self is everything, and the core healing skills of Schema Therapy will give you just that. Just keep at it. This makes me think of one of my longer-term clients, who has made leaps and bounds in her approach to dating by using Schema Therapy. She used to struggle with low self-worth and denied her sensitivity and vulnerability. My reflections that her emotional sensitivity and vulnerability were a beautiful part of her true nature begun to sink in. She worked to truly love and accept this part of herself, and see her softness as her biggest gift. When this belief shifted, immediately, she attracted dates who valued her clear communication and her feelings. Her boundaries strengthened and allowed her to receive the treatment she truly deserved. Her relationship with herself guided her dating choices.

Everything I say here is a guide and you really need to be within the personal context of the therapy room to truly choose the best path for you. I have seen troubled relationship dynamics shift in several sessions, and others are not salvageable because so much individual healing is needed.

Your schemas are your roadmap to dating, partner choice, and the intimacy you bring into your life. And your schemas are the bumps that can show up in relationships down the track. You must begin to change how you talk to yourself, you must change how you express yourself in your relationships, and I deeply believe that you must choose partners who do not reinforce these patterns. And if you're living in a relationship that does reinforce these patterns, I recommend you seek out professional help to provide some clarity.

I remember being on a first coffee date with a man I'd met online. He was introverted, reserved and I felt unsure of his interest in me. He was talking about his family, and I asked a follow up question to show interest. He seemed to close off somewhat and then redirected the conversation to a more superficial topic. I knew instantly that we were not a match. And so, when he reached out again, I declined his invitation with certainty, knowing that I would risk feeling alone and unseen with a man like this. His wall was up, and I suspected he saw emotions as unnecessary at best and a sign of weakness at worst. This would surely reinforce my emotional deprivation, fear of abandonment and shame schemas. It might sound dramatic to not proceed with a second date, but I did this with confidence. I had a clear, strong relationship with myself, and was happy to be in my own company until I met someone who could add to my life.

My Go-To Core Skills For Healing

Below are skills to help you to think differently, feel differently, and behave differently, depending on your schemas. Begin to view yourself as a detective; a truth-seeker who challenges the unhelpful thoughts that have kept you stuck for a long time, to find personal freedom. Do intentionally seek new experiences which facilitate healing and prevent you blocking love.

Fear of Abandonment Schema
If you have a fear of abandonment schema, you are likely to believe you will be left. Instead, think about the times when someone has shown you consistency and reliability. Learn to tolerate reasonable

periods of being alone and avoid clinging, and stop driving your relationships forward by pursuing, or getting angry or punishing. You must learn to warmly and assertively communicate your anxiety to your partner. You should assess and reflect upon your partner choice, and work to choose a partner who is emotionally responsive.

Failure Schema

If you think you are a failure, think about any achievements you've made, however small. You must absolutely celebrate those and know that they matter. You must also learn to take risks and be willing to have a go despite your worries. You are likely to surprise yourself.

Defectiveness/ Shame Schema

If you have this schema and think you are unworthy of love, think about your qualities that make you worthwhile, even if they feel fleeting. Grasp on to any thoughts about your goodness.

Extend love and compassion to all of you, especially the parts you don't like. You must cultivate the emotion of love which is opposite to shame. Here are some ideas on how to cultivate the emotions of love and worth. Work on spending more time with those who make you feel loved and internally remind yourself of the love they have for you in that moment—stay present and engaged to their connection. Get out your journal, and sit and write a loving letter to your younger self. Find a quiet spot, close your eyes, and visualise yourself as a child. Perhaps give her a hug, and remind her of her worth.

Self-Sacrifice Schema

Protect your energy, especially if your schema is self-sacrifice. Close your eyes, and visualise your energy within you. Perhaps it sits in a particular place in your body, or has a particular feeling, colour or shape. It is a precious resource. Picture it being protected by the boundaries of your body. You will feel lighter and brighter when this energy is protected and given wisely.

Mistrust/Abuse Schema

Learn to more accurately assess a potential partner's ability to be open, reliable and vulnerable. This will require you to be open and vulnerable, so that you give your partner clear messages that you want to cultivate and develop trust. By sitting back and remaining closed off you are not facilitating trust, you are preventing it. Assess a person's character over time.

Emotional Deprivation Schema

Choose to be open and vulnerable from the beginning, and disclose your needs and feelings, so that you can allow your partner to show up for you. Avoid participating in your emotional deprivation by holding back and punishing a partner for not reading your mind. You can work to gently and kindly guide your partner towards your needs, rather than holding things in. If you find your vulnerability is not being met or received across time, however, assess this with the help of someone you trust, such as a therapist. You will only heal with an emotionally reciprocal relationship.

Emotional Inhibition Schema

You must practice naming and observing your emotions as they arise, and practice talking from your heart rather than your head.

Repatterning For Love

If you avoid sharing your feelings when there is conflict, you risk your partner viewing you as uncaring. Try a daily emotional check-in and see what you notice inside your body, or consider attending a therapy group which will help you open up emotionally.

This list is far from exhaustive, however, I do hope it begins to provide the first stepping stones for you. A way to think differently, feel differently, and behave differently, and to stop schemas blocking you from having the love you long for and deserve. Ultimately, you must shift your schemas at three levels: cognitive, emotive, and behavioural.

EXERCISE
Embodying Healing

Consider what we've discussed in this chapter and journal or think about the statements below:

The more loving, healthy, and helpful beliefs that I need to cultivate are:

The emotions that I need to embody more of are:

Repatterning For Love

I will embody this emotion through the practice of (consider imagery, writing, and actions):

The behaviours that I want to work on shifting are:

CHAPTER SEVEN
Attachment is Everything

Upon reflection, I had always been drawn to a particular type of partner—partners that failed to provide me with the sense of emotional security that I needed. Whether it was their own emotional disturbances, low self-worth, lack of life direction or an unsettled sense of belonging, it all culminated in the same feeling: paralysing anxiety.

I had tended to unconsciously select partners who were emotionally intense, needy, and immature, and under stress they tended to withdraw from the relationship and into their work, substances (drugs, food), and even other relationships (sex with strangers). Several of my partners had their own wounds (defectiveness and entitlement schemas precisely) and, when conflict ensued, I rarely felt reassured, soothed or secure. In fact, I felt alone, abandoned, rejected, and unworthy of their love. And I would berate myself for my emotional neediness.

My anxiety would often skyrocket, as I was the one left stranded desperately pursuing closeness, resolution, and reconnection, and they stayed further and further away. I still feel pain as I remember a partner who failed to reply to several desperate messages for seventy-two hours.

My relationships often started with me feeling special and adored, and relatively quickly my emotional need for closeness pushed my partners further away. I struggled to understand how they could do this to me.

I want to take you back in time to a relationship that opened up my attachment wounds. It took place several years before the big breakup of this book. A hurt bigger than any I've ever felt, bigger than the hurt of breaking up with the man you are going to marry. I'll explain why.

The lowest moment of my life was the first and only time a partner had left me. I had always been the one to end relationships, so I was utterly unprepared for this. I can't even say he broke up with me—the words were never uttered. After some months of dating a beautiful Italian man, we decided to move in together. I liked his vitality, warmth, and European ways. I felt like my life was a dream, as I hopped on the back of his scooter, and he drove us to the beach in summer. He invited me to Italy during his vacation, and I was to join him once he had been there a few weeks, and I could take leave from work.

I never made it to Italy. Once he was there, his phone calls became less, and things just felt 'off'. I was anxious, angry, distressed and confused. He'd blame it on the reception. I was even questioning the reception in Italy, because I wanted to believe him. (I travelled to Italy some years later and I can report that their mobile reception is just fine). I wasn't getting any reassurance, and he eventually revealed that he would need to move back home. We had only just moved in together, so you can imagine my devastation. I just couldn't get on the plane to meet him—my soul was destroyed. *Bella Italia* became *Brutta Italia*.

I plunged into the worst episode of depression in my life, faced with sleepless nights, and crying in my car as I attempted to drive to work. Most days I made it. To this day, I have still not received the money he owed me for the furniture we purchased together for the home. He was going to pay me back due to his holiday expenses. So yes, I have been burnt, romantically and financially, by putting my needs last. I tell you this story because it provides insight into fear of abandonment and the pain that being left can cause. I want every person to understand their attachment wounds so that they don't drive your relationship choices, unconsciously.

WTF is Attachment Trauma?

After years of therapy and self-reflection, it is clear to me I have Attachment Trauma. Attachment Trauma refers to the wounds left upon us by our primary caregivers, the first figures we bond with. My belief is that most of us do, and the sooner we understand it, the better. Both Schema Therapy and understanding Attachment Theory have helped me identify my core wounds and been instrumental in my healing, and I wish you the same profound healing.

So, what is Attachment Theory? Developed by psychiatrist John Bowlby, who was interested in understanding infant distress when separated from their caregivers, the theory describes incredibly well how we bond and connect with important figures in our lives. Later, it was expanded by developmental research psychologist Mary Ainsworth who studied the attachment relationship between infants and their primary caregivers, particularly mothers.

It turns out that the way in which we bond with and feel soothed by our caregiver carries over and translates into our adult romantic relationships. The model we received early in life contributes to how we behave in our romantic relationships. It is true: the roots of our adult relationship distress are in childhood! Let's see how this all plays out.

Secure Attachment

Childhood: A securely attached individual has tended to experience reliability, predictability, safety and security from their caregiver, and trusts that they can reach out to them in a time of need. Such individuals grow up with an innate sense of self-worth, feeling worthy of love from others, and trusting in the goodness of others.

Adulthood: Because they have experienced attunement and interest from others, they tend to be vulnerable, warm, open, secure in themselves, trusting of others, and approach relationships with a willingness to communicate, share with, and support each other. They have realistic expectations of relationships; that issues are to be worked through and do not mean the end of the relationship. Such individuals tend to have an easier time with romantic and intimate relationships.

Anxious Attachment

Childhood: Whereas in an anxiously attached individual, they are more likely to have experienced an emotionally unavailable or unpredictable caregiver who was emotionally needy themselves, intrusive or overprotective. Their caregiver may have been warm and affectionate at times, and then more emotionally closed off or withdrawn, contributing to the child developing a more shaky sense of security in another.

Adulthood: An anxiously attached individual can become highly distressed when there is conflict or distance in a relationship, and can become clingy and pursuing of their partner. They may excessively text a partner, demand reassurance, or feel anger which appears out of proportion to partners -all stemming from their anxiety about the future of the relationship. Such individuals may repress emotions for a long time and fear that they are too much. Anxiously attached individuals tend to worry that their relationship won't last and fear they are 'not enough' in some way. They can take on a huge burden of responsibility for relationship failures.

Avoidant Attachment
Childhood: Avoidantly attached individuals tend to have experienced a parent who was misattuned to their emotional needs or even shamed the expression of emotions. Achievement was valued above emotional and mental wellbeing, and created distance between child and caregiver.

Adulthood: As such, avoidantly attached individuals can feel overwhelmed by emotional closeness and the needs of their partner. Emotional closeness in adult romantic relationships feels unfamiliar at best, and scary at worst. Such individuals tend to withdraw when there is conflict and struggle to share their inner world with their partner for fear of making things worse. The most common sentiments of an avoidantly attached partner that I have heard over and over again in my therapy room is that 'I'm never enough' for my partner. Avoidantly attached partners may deeply struggle with vulnerability and affection, and to have trust in others.

Fearful Avoidant Attachment
Childhood: those with this style of attachment tended to experience a caregiver whom they feared, creating much internal confusion for the child.

Adulthood: Adults with this attachment style can present with the feelings and behaviours of both anxious and avoidant attachment. They both long for intimacy and fear it and may anticipate rejection.

Please note, I do not believe that you need to be securely attached yourself or need to find a securely attached partner in order to have a happy and healthy relationship. I have worked with couples who had been told by their previous therapist that they were not compatible due to their match of anxious and avoidant attachment styles, and should separate. I was as upset as they were that this was the message told to them. You simply need a dose of understanding, compassion, respect, and willingness to communicate to bridge the gap.

Overcoming Fear of Abandonment

My dating life was gathering momentum, and I was actively chatting to potential matches. When I met a lovely, young, single father in person, I was touched by his warmth. He was clearly grounded, calm and secure in himself. My 'urge to merge' kicked in because he seemed 'perfect'—sensitive, thoughtful, heartfelt. That meant on my second date, I presented as nervous and overly invested, and upon reflection, I'm quite sure that terrified the guy. Fear of abandonment is more likely to wreak havoc when you begin to like someone. You may notice yourself idealising them. The more you like them, the more you tend to pursue and overwhelm them, out of fear of things not moving forward. I was truly gutted when he didn't get in touch after our second date, and I should have let it be. I was still learning the importance of reciprocal interest, and his final text let me know he did not wish to take things further. There was still plenty of healing work to be done, which I'll explain here.

A deep-seated fear of abandonment is common in many of my female clients, and has roots in their childhoods where they experienced physical and emotional neglect. The little girl inside of them is still longing for closeness and connection, and the reliable presence of another. And without conscious awareness that little girl ('inner child') is driving your connection-seeking behaviour. The good news is we can put adult you back into the driver's seat.

We take charge of fear of abandonment by ultimately realising that you will never be alone because you (healthy adult, grown up you) will never leave you (the scared little girl inside of you). Having this realisation and framework for healing radically transformed my life, my connection to myself, and how I dated. It gave me the confidence to date and ride the bumps of the journey to ultimately finding my partner because I had new found trust in myself to soothe myself and show up for me.

I am an empowered, self-sufficient, self-soothing woman who ultimately cares for myself. And a loving connection to yourself becomes the model for the relationships you seek: ones that are built on presence, reliability, vulnerability and intimacy.

So, where do you start when you fear abandonment? It's important that you start with yourself, by going inwards and soothing yourself, and your inner child. You can then turn towards others for support. Here's what I suggest:

1. Begin to notice when fear of abandonment is triggered and the feelings that arise in your body. For example, do you feel anxious when a date doesn't get in contact, or do you start to worry that things won't work out with your new partner when they haven't yet replied to your text?
2. Identify the origins of your fear of abandonment story. Think about memories in your history that have ultimately cultivated a fear of abandonment. Remind yourself of the narrative of your younger self's pain.
3. Validate your fear and anxiety as it arises, for example: *It makes so much sense that you fear them leaving you, because in your family your mum also wasn't always there for you.*
4. Validate your longings for connection: *It's so okay that you long for the presence of another right now; that is human.*
5. Reassure yourself that you are a connection to your vulnerable part: *I'm here for you right now, and I'll listen to how you feel.*
6. Bring in some healthy adult wisdom and hope: *Even though you may feel alone or scared right now, I know this will pass.*
7. If you have a partner, be brave and courageous, and reach out to them, asking for what you need.

There's also an Inner Child Imagery exercise included in the appendix to support your healing and connecting to self (see page 237).

I used the above skills over and over when I was dating, particularly for times when I didn't hear from the new object of my affection, and needed reassurance and comfort. With time and practice, I learnt I was able to show up for myself and didn't need to rely on others for comfort and connection. Ultimately, this loving connection that I was fostering with myself and my inner child wounds facilitated developing a loving connection with others too, based on compassion and calm.

Fear of abandonment can ultimately be healed, as can an anxious or avoidant attachment style. We must ultimately identify our tendencies or struggles, work on soothing ourselves and practice vulnerable self-expression, as well as date with clarity and choose partners that offer a sense of security. And don't forget, security can always be cultivated with a willing partner.

Of course, finding a secure partner isn't a magic pill to all your personal hurdles. In our next chapter, we'll cover a big one—shame and how to overcome it. In my professional opinion, the shame that lurks within us is what holds many women back from relationship fulfilment—and I'm on a personal mission to change that.

If You're Wondering, Are Our Attachment Styles Incompatible?

One of the most interesting observations about this attachment stuff: more anxiously attached partners tend to partner up with avoidantly attached partners, which in turn tends to exaggerate the existing attachment pattern of each: the anxiously attached partner feels anxious with distancing and withdrawal, and is longing for their partner to return and offer security; however, the more avoidantly attached partner can feel overwhelmed by their more anxiously attached partner's emotions and can feel like they never get it right for their partner, hence retreating further and further away. There is definitely a way forward with the right help and support so that you can understand and honour each other's needs and way of being.

EXERCISE
Cultivating Security

Consider what we've covered in the chapter above, and journal or think about these questions:

What relationship events are likely to trigger your fear of abandonment? Map this on to earlier life events.

Secure relationships are cultivated. How would you behave if you trusted in the security of your relationship?

If you feel anxious about your (potential) partner pulling away from you, what self-dialogue could you use to soothe yourself? Use the above section to guide you.

CHAPTER EIGHT

The Shame That Lurks Within

It is certainly more comfortable for us to believe that we actually like ourselves or love ourselves. In a world oversaturated by self-help literature touting the importance of self-love, there's plenty of reasons to deny any deficiency in self-love. As a professional helping others work on their own shame, I liked to think that I did truly love and accept myself as I was. In fact, I hoped that I modelled healthy self-esteem to my clients. I wasn't actively in denial about my low self-worth, I was blinded to it.

I was continuing to date, hoping to find a partner, equally wondering at times if it would happen for me. Despite these worries, I continued to meet matches who appeared hopeful. However, there were healing lessons I still needed to have. When I delved more deeply into my wounds on this more recent journey of self-discovery, it became clear that my relationship history pointed to significant gaps in my self-worth. There were subtle clues that I didn't value myself enough in the treatment I had accepted from past partners, however, I was really out of touch with this painful part of myself. Was I proud of who I was, and all that I had achieved? Did I think I was a good person? Whilst I could answer 'yes' to those questions, my relationship self-worth was still at rock-bottom.

In reality my relationship self-worth told the story of a woman who didn't truly believe she was enough as she was: I didn't believe I deserved the type of healthy and reciprocal love that I longed for, and I believed I needed to do more or be more in order to be loved. Precisely, I believed I was worthy of love only if I cared for and gave of myself to a partner, and I gravitated towards unhealthy male partners who I felt needed me rather than chose me because of my innate worth. I also believed deep down that I was emotionally difficult and that I had to be wary of overexpressing myself and my needs.

I historically worked terribly hard to repair conflict where I felt I had been too emotional and contributed to my partner feeling terrible about themselves. I over-functioned emotionally and it often felt like what I did, and who I was, was never enough. I felt constantly exhausted by working hard to be good: to be extra kind, encouraging, other-focused, sweet, loving, agreeable, low maintenance and 'together'.

Shame lurked inside of me rendering me to give more of myself. I deeply wish my younger self knew she was enough. I wish she had known what to accept, how to have boundaries, and how to give more love to herself.

So, here is my truth. Whilst I liked parts of myself, I was not at all comfortable with my more vulnerable parts. I wasn't comfortable with my sensitivity, emotions and needs, and did acrobats trying to suppress those very human parts of me. I was also a lot more comfortable with being in a giving role, and I wasn't at ease with the idea that I should receive from my relationships.

Repatterning For Love

I functioned in relationships by focusing on all the love and help I could give to my partner; how I could enrich their lives, solve their problems and be the best I could be for them. The fact that I didn't consider my own emotional wellbeing a priority suggests a deficit in self-worth. I had never faced the possibility of my own shame before.

At this point, it had been months since my ex-partner and I had broken up. I had continued exploring my relationship challenges in therapy. I had been attending sessions regularly, unpacking fear of abandonment and my family of origin story. I distinctly remember one session when, out of the blue whilst processing some fears, I noticed a different sensation in my body—one that I'd certainly never sat with before.

It was a deep, aching, heavy feeling in the pit of my stomach. Hiding underneath sensations of anxiety, tingling worries, and fears of being abandoned and alone in the world, was a feeling I hadn't recognised within me before. The feeling was undeniably shame, and it took me by surprise. I remember the confusion of noticing that feeling. I had always subscribed to my own narrative that said I liked myself, who I was, and what I stood for. And whilst that was all true, I was deeply uneasy and uncomfortable with several parts of myself. The self-illusion had shattered, and now I had to face my shame.

I felt shame for being single and alone. I felt shame for not knowing how to navigate relationships and I felt shame because of partners abandoning me. I had shame because I deeply felt that I had been abandoned because there was something wrong with me; that I wasn't enough in some way. It was the conclusion I had come to because of my relationship disasters, and in fact, it was the belief of my inner child, my younger self.

When Will It Happen For Me

When I did the inner work to break my shame down, it looked like this:

- ♥ I had deep wounds of feeling unworthy of love because my role was to give love rather than receive love.
- ♥ I had wounds of shame because I felt ashamed of my emotions, and worried that they were too much for others, that I was too needy.
- ♥ I had wounds of shame because I had accepted unacceptable treatment and deprioritised myself.
- ♥ I had shame because I had learnt along the way to silence myself as my voice didn't really matter.

For the first time in my life, I realised and then accepted that I did carry shame and that I needed to address it. Even if my head knew that I was worthy of love, my heart and body weren't as easily convinced. This is the work of therapy: to shift what your head knows to be true into a felt experience in your body. It is not enough to know you are worthy of love, you must feel that in your body and heart.

Here's what I've discovered. Before dispelling shame, it really needs to be acknowledged. The origins of your shame (defectiveness schema) must truly be understood. You can't sweep shame away by minimising your past or the events that contributed to the development of shame. Your shame must be felt and it must be experienced through the eyes of younger, child you.

Shame breeds in secrecy, and so, the other antidote to shame is sharing. And this is why I share my story. Perhaps my story has parallels to your own and helps further normalise rather than stigmatise your experiences with love.

The Origins of Our Shame Stories

If you have ever feared being abandoned by your partner, it is quite likely you carry shame. As little children we have not yet developed the maturity and mental acuity to understand the complexity of life or the complexity of our own caregivers and their trauma. And so, what do little ones do when they fear abandonment from a caregiver? They develop a narrative of self-blame because they can control their behaviours and actions and restore connection to their attachment figure; that is, because of this blame and shame children often work harder to be more kind, gentle, patient, easy-going, independent, hardworking and achieving.

Children crave connection, security, and attachment from a caregiver and that longing propels them to develop coping strategies to get that fundamental need for love met. You can see how this fear of rejection or abandonment from a caregiver incites action, so we strive to become more of something (good or easy), and less of something else (difficult or challenging), rather than being simply ourselves. Think of little you, or your inner child, and the narrative she developed about herself because of her conditioning. See if you can place together the puzzle pieces of her shame narrative.

If you are like many of the women I work with, you very likely have your own shame story that started when you were very young, and has followed you around. Your shame story may have lurked in the shadows undetected for years, like my own, or it may have been louder and unrelenting, like the internalised voice of a critical parent, or a persistent and cruel tormentor. I want to help you understand exactly what shame is, and how shame can be healed.

Healing from shame is a bumpy and almost life-long journey (not to scare you!), so you should be realistic with the speed at which you rediscover your self-worth. Whilst some level of self-doubt or insecurity may always remain (and that is totally okay), it is my hope that your shame story is balanced with more self-love, self-care, self-compassion, and self-respect. Perhaps that each day you are more accepting of yourself than the day before, and some days, you can send some love back to yourself. Let's start with understanding shame some more and then move towards how we heal shame.

Sticky, Sickly Shame

Shame can sometimes be misunderstood. Simply, shame is the feeling of heaviness we experience when we feel bad, defective, flawed, worthless or unlovable in some way. Shame is associated with feeling inferior to, less than, or beneath others. We experience feelings of shame when others turn away and disconnect from us, as this disconnection sends us the message that we are not worthy of another's time, love, patience, energy, or care.

Shame also feels incredibly lonely and isolating because we are cast out or aside, often for simply being ourselves. Being shamed can have huge consequences for one's mental health and emotional wellbeing and can trigger depression, overwhelming pain and sadness. Receiving too many messages in life about our lack of value or importance can be deeply painful and scary because, if we aren't important to another, we face being alone in the world. Our survival and self-worth depends on reliable connection to others, and ideally, we are accepted for who we are rather than conditionally. Sadly, too many of us have received love that is conditional, which only reinforces shame and low self-worth. It is truly a precious gift to be loved exactly as you are.

Repatterning For Love

I am reminded of one of my clients who had been in an anxiety-inducing on and off relationship, where she suspected that her partner had cheated on her and eventually left her for another woman. Her shame was both sticky and sickly.

Sticky Shame: My client's shame was sticky in that it was an incredible force, beating her up and criticising her in every way possible. The torment was endless. Her inner critic was significant, and she ruminated and replayed her past actions under a magnifying glass daily. She frequently asked in sessions what if she did more? Would he have stayed? I clearly told her no; it was not about doing more or being more in some way.

Sickly Shame: Her shame was sickly because it was leading her down a dark, treacherous path to depression, and she was at risk of losing perspective on her self-worth. However, it is true for this client, like the rest of us, that her shame story went way back into childhood. I wasn't going to let her get absorbed by her shame. Fortunately, I had done my own shame work and had plenty of tools in my kit.

Through my own learnings in Schema Therapy, I had learnt that the only way to shrink shame was to replace the space it occupied with love. Just as love is the answer to a lot of things in life, love is the antidote to shame—but what does it really look like in practice?

The Antidote To Shame Is Love

So, we've all heard the cliché that you need to love yourself before you love someone else. Is that really true? My answer is yes, and no. Yes, because you need a good dose of self-love as a foundation to ride the bumps of dating and relationship triggers. No, because, loving yourself is truly a lifelong journey, and the love of another certainly helps with this. So how do we strike the balance between loving ourselves but still making space for the love of another?

A healthy love provides us with many gifts including shelter, safety, security, nurturing, acceptance, and empowerment. Love is the base from which we thrive in life. However, most of the clients I work with that have deep-seated shame, struggle to love themselves. The healing road is long and bumpy, but ultimately worthwhile.

We heal shame when we can show up exactly as we are. We need to find places and spaces in life where we feel we can be ourselves, free from fear of judgment. We need to often shed the conditioning of the past and shed the child-like coping styles of fitting in. It is time to stop fitting in for the sake of others. Love does not require you to fit in. True love requires you to be yourself.

As we have done earlier on, you must continue to reflect on what happened to your younger self in the family you grew up in, and consider the messages she did or did not receive about her lovability:

- ♥ Was she ever shamed, shunned, ostracised, or turned away from in a time of need?
- ♥ Did she long for somebody to feel proud of her, or to ask about how she was feeling on a hard day?
- ♥ Did she long for more time, energy, or presence from her caregiver?
- ♥ Think about 'teenager you' and her emotional world, or how she felt about her physical body and abilities. And then connect these experiences to the beliefs that were formed within adult you, who then entered relationships with these stories about her worth and lovability.

Repatterning For Love

Ultimately, you must remind the little girl within you that she received messages about herself and that she is so much more than the messages she received. You must also remind yourself that the love you received or didn't receive from others is a product of their own conditioning or trauma, rather than being about how truly loveable she was and is now.

I think most of us are truly more loving to others than we are to ourselves. And most of us inherently know, believe and feel in our hearts that all children are worthy of love. We love children simply because they are here; we love their unique nature, spirit, and temperament.

We do not love little children because of what they do for us, we simply love. And it is vital that we do not disconnect from children when they are expressing emotions. We accept them and nurture them as they are. This is the lens that I want you to see yourself through, it is a lens of pure acceptance and love. We will touch on this more later on in the book, but for now, try to bring to mind an image of younger you, and see if you can notice any warmth in your body as you think about her and what she went through.

When I began getting acquainted with my own shame, I faced blocks and resistance to self-love and finding love, as you may do too. My shame presented challenges to dating and beyond. I felt I was walking a tightrope, swaying between my old and new life. My shame would pull me back into old thinking habits and told me that I didn't deserve a capable partner, that I needed to prove my worth through giving, and that I should make allowances when dating. These thought patterns intensified when I was rejected in dating.

Fortunately, through therapy, I was also connecting with my younger self, and with that lens I was able to lovingly rediscover my innate worth. I knew my younger self deserved so much love and care. Surely, if she did, so did adult me.

Part of me felt like a fraud for turning away certain men due to their lack of stability, however, the other part of me knew I needed to intentionally seek a partner who was sure of who he was and where he was going in life. My shame nearly sabotaged my dating choices, and had me persist when there was a lack of interest. It nearly stopped me from sharing how I felt and declaring what I really wanted from a relationship, for fear I would be perceived as needy. However, I kept trusting in what I was learning in therapy, and practiced sharing these exact needs as I dated. With intentional effort, the shame was shrinking.

As I was growing, so too were my clients in therapy. As I reminded them of the love they truly deserved, I knew I deserved this too. As I validated their emotions, I equally validated my own.

Shame can also make us slip up if we're in a relationship. If you are within a relationship, you want to avoid sinking into a shame spiral each time your partner gives you feedback in your relationship. It is important that you can separate a partner's need or request from your self-worth and know that you are loveable and worthwhile in the face of relationship conflict. For example, if your partner gives feedback that you hurt them, accept what you can from that feedback. Their feedback doesn't mean you are a bad person, it means you're human. See if you can acknowledge their feelings and repair what you can.

Can you allow yourself to be a good person who upsets your partner on occasions? Can you accept that your emotions get the better of you at times? Your own self-love and ability to shrink shame will ultimately lead you to a more loving relationship with a partner. This has been my story, it is the story of many women

Repatterning For Love

I have worked with, and it can be your story too. I wish you the courage to show up fully as the beautiful being that you are—with emotions, volume, boundaries, imperfections, and your unfiltered personality.

EXERCISE
Healing Shame

Consider what we've covered in this chapter and journal or take a few moments to think about these questions—you might even want to discuss them with your friends, siblings or your partner.

Where do you think your shame comes from? Consider memories across your life.

What is something you could say to yourself to remind yourself that your shame messages are conditioning, rather than reality?

Repatterning For Love

What loving messages did you wish that younger you received?

Think of your loving nature with others. Name some ways in which you could treat yourself with the same love and care.

PART THREE

Seeking Love

CHAPTER NINE

Dating With Eyes Wide Open

So far, I have taken you on a journey of self-understanding and rewiring your wounds so that you are equipped to either date with confidence, assess your current relationship health, or deepen your connection with your current partner. I hope that the above chapters have provided you with an enhanced understanding of the origins of your wounds and how to begin healing them. May you now be more equipped than ever before with skills to show up in life with authenticity, backed by a healthy dose of self-love and self-compassion. This work is ongoing across our lives, and if you stick with it, the growth and change you long for will be yours.

Even if you are within a relationship currently, there is still value in this section of the book, so I urge you to read it all. Here I will cover understanding the art of dating as well as connecting more deeply as your relationship progresses. This section will also be useful if you are questioning your current relationship and wondering if it has what it takes to last the distance. You will be able to consider what to keep, and what needs updating within yourself, your partner, or the relationship.

When Will It Happen For Me

Has anyone ever taught you how to date, let alone choose a partner, beyond cliched advice? In fact, my experience was that I received a lack of advice about dating and just learnt on the go. And look where I ended up. Now, there is almost an over-supply of relationship and dating advice online and, so, it is confusing as to what advice to hold on to and which to reject.

More recently, one of the women in a women's group boldly stated that the relationship lessons I teach in the program should be part of the school curriculum, and I tend to agree. If we learnt earlier in life how to navigate dating and relationships, and learnt how to choose people who are trustworthy, kind, and reliable, perhaps, we could have avoided a lot of our relational pain. It's never too late to learn, as I learnt on my personal journey. And I've got your back going forward.

Given all my previous dating and relationship blunders, I had an inner knowing that if I was to date, I had to do it very differently to how I had ever done it before. It was December, and I was much stronger within myself after several months of cultivating a life on my own terms and seriously prioritising my needs and feelings. I was a mix of fragile, realistically tentative, and also excited about dating. I had a three-month-old puppy, my new best friend, by my side. A client recently told me about a TikTok meme she saw that said behind every anxious girl is an anxious dog. This was true for me. The companionship of my puppy gave me such love and security, and I for her.

In this period of my life, I was devouring self-help books and following dating and relationship gurus to figure it all out. I had scoured the internet for all I could find on dating and attachment theory, determined to do it right this time. By 'it', I meant choosing a suitable partner and finding love. I felt armed and ready ... relatively.

Seeking Love

Dating was both scary and exciting for me, as it is for many women, complete with hope and disappointment. Trust me, I do understand why the idea of dating can be terrifying, having been there myself, and heard countless women's dating fears and stories.

I can recall the stories of two women I worked with who had mistrust schemas. They worried that they would miss clues about someone they would date and end up with an unhealthy partner who would cause them emotional harm. They worried about being stuck with a partner that wasn't right for them, and then blame themselves for ending up in a toxic relationship.

My personal worries were similar. I had two fears: that I would end up choosing an emotionally needy or unstable partner again and have another relationship failure, or I wouldn't meet anyone at all, and be sad and alone forever. Fortunately, my story has a happy ending, just like that of many of my clients. Dating is really so very triggering for those of us with attachment wounds and brings up fears of abandonment, worries about being defective, unworthy, unattractive, or triggers preoccupations about not being able to trust in another altogether. Some of us may be so anxious about dating that we avoid it altogether. The good news is that there are simple and effective strategies you can use immediately to date with more confidence and a lot less anxiety.

This is what I like to call 'dating with eyes wide open'. If you regularly check-in with your dating experiences, reflect, and journal, you are way more likely to stay on track. I was very serious about having a plan and a set of guidelines to help me with my partner choice, given that I'd never had what I considered a truly healthy relationship before. You should be just as serious and diligent.

We need to know what to look out for and what to avoid. What is worth persisting with, and what requires moving on. If it wasn't for this plan, I truly don't think I would have found my current partner, and chosen so well. So read on for more on how to do this.

Dating Doesn't Suck

Now, just because I had a plan, it doesn't mean I was a star student of dating. What I did do well however, was to give dating a chance over and over, and over again. I ask you to do the same so you can develop your search criteria, self-awareness, and growth.

I initially decided to start with what I viewed to be more serious websites. Why? I thought I was being more deliberate, opting for a pool of people who were taking dating seriously and paying for a premium service. I was also still healing and anti-apps for some time, as I had met my ex-partner there and my self-protection was kicking in. What I now know with certainty is it matters less which platform or app you use when you have skills to screen potential matches and are clear on who you are and what you're looking for.

I dated one match who I initiated contact with for about two months and even though it ended, I am grateful for that experience. He treated me kindly, was intelligent and hardworking, but ultimately not ready to share his life with someone. Dating this man, who had some avoidant attachment tendencies, was also so helpful for me, as it gave me the opportunity to practice self-soothing my anxiety and having important and vulnerable conversations with him.

I hope you can, and I encourage you to, view dating through this lens—that it provides a rich opportunity for self-learning and growth. If this is your lens, then dating doesn't have to suck so much. Reminding yourself of your values for personal growth may assist in riding the emotional waves of dating.

I know as well as you that dating is not pain-free. Whether it is wasting time meeting those who aren't actually interested in pursuing a relationship, or having to endure the date who only talks about themselves, or defames their ex-partner. Or the sheer exhaustion of being polite and engaging, investing time in conversations, only to be ghosted online, or worse still, have this happen in real life.

Please remember this is not a 'you thing', it's definitely a 'them thing'. And, for the women who've had bad date after bad date, or heartbreak after heartbreak, I want to offer a heartfelt acknowledgement of your courage in the pursuit of love. It's okay to take a break if you need it; however, please don't avoid it altogether if love is what you truly long for. I believe we must take action in the direction of our dreams.

Dating 'Appily!

I have heard countless stories from all genders, from inside and outside the therapy room, telling of someone meeting their much-adored partner online. If it's used as a compliment to your life, to add to your chances of meeting your future mate, then I say go for it.

Whilst I've met many clients who view online dating as cringey or embarrassing, or alternatively, they long to meet someone naturally, I encourage you to open your heart and mind. I had to put aside my misconceptions when I ventured onto 'The Apps' but I was willing to do so and try to not take it too seriously.

When Will It Happen For Me

We live in a very different generation to that of our parents. Our world is even more fast-paced and disconnected than before. I struggled to meet men in real-life and I love that these apps can provide opportunities to meet a potential partner. As an introvert who works in a female dominated profession, my opportunities to meet suitable suitors were scarce.

There are plenty of ways to increase your odds of meeting someone besides apps—get out into the world and say 'yes' to invites and catch-ups. There is, however, also a place for the online dating marketplace, especially because it can put less pressure on your schedule and your wallet. Of course, as with anything online, safety matters—trust your instincts, set boundaries, and take precautions when meeting someone new.

Here's what I suggest to ensure your experience with online dating doesn't suck:

- ♥ **Be crystal clear:** It is important that your dating profile describes you, your values, your life, and what you are looking for in detail. You are not doing yourself any favours if you are muted, generic, and unspecific about what you want. Being crystal clear, expressive, and vulnerable about your intentions will speed up the process of finding your mate. Whilst you may get fewer matches, you will get more suitable matches. Think about showing your warmth, your interests, and describe yourself as your loved ones and friends describe you. I think of the brave women I have worked with who proudly updated their profiles to show more of themselves—being clear on wanting a long-term relationship, a nurturing partner, and a life of adventure.

Seeking Love

- ♥ **Know your goals:** In general, I advise only pursuing matches who clearly state on their profile that they are also seeking a long-term relationship. My current partner did not actually state his relationship preference when I first saw his profile, and I nearly swiped left. However, I swiped right because he said he was able to, 'listen to you whinge about Karen after a hard day at work', and I love a good listener. He turned out to be humorous, playful, and also a good listener who cares about my struggles, all good relationship qualities. There are clues in the profiles.
- ♥ **Go beyond the app:** Whilst profiles are illuminating, they don't always show exactly who someone is; it's important to get a feel by chatting, perhaps a phone call before meeting, and moving off the app to a date relatively quickly (within a week or two). One of my clients is now also dating a man she met online and showed me his profile—it was clearly warm, engaging, and also showed his relational qualities. Keep swiping till you find your match. I've worked with women where the process can take months or years, however, eventually, they get there, and you can too. So, now that we have covered how to approach the dating apps, lets discuss how to collate dating data so you can be in the driver's seat of your dating decisions.

Dating Diligently

As you have perhaps now come to realise, many of us date blindly. We have simply dated based on how we feel, rather than truly considered what we are looking for. In addition, you may also have dated from a place of unrecognised and unhealed wounds, tending towards partners that reinforce hurt and pain, rather than allowing you to feel safe and secure in love.

Journaling was absolutely critical in my dating journey, as it facilitated listening to my heart and body. I collected data on when I felt at ease or when I became anxious and agitated in the presence of another, and it helped me figure out the root of these feelings, whether my own stuff was coming up or I was unsafe with a particular person. Your body feeling consistently settled in the presence of another is a huge giveaway that a person is good for you. All partners ultimately can trigger us, but a feeling of calm with another is what to aim for.

After each date, I did a values check-in, an emotions check-in, and a general summary of my experiences with that person: what I liked or was unsure about, the flow of the conversation, their ability to talk about others with kindness and with some level of vulnerability.

Dedicated to my mission, I kept dating and journaling, holding hope, and learning to trust my intuition again by listening to my body. A few months into my dating journey, I just wasn't clicking with the men I had met so far. After many unfruitful dates, I switched over to another app. Why not change strategies or revamp your approach if things aren't working?

After about five months of dating, I matched with someone who felt different. His profile was warm and engaging, and as we began chatting, I appreciated his curiosity and interest in me. His questions demonstrated he was serious about entering a relationship, and was sussing things out. Before we met, he asked about my communication needs within a relationship; his text asked:

Seeking Love

'Are you the type of person that likes to hear from your partner each day?' A question that was pleasantly surprising and hopeful!

I'll never forget getting home from a first date with the guy who felt different. I was filled with warmth because I knew I'd just met a nice human. He had taken me to his favourite Mexican restaurant close to the city. He was very funny, warm, and treated the waiter with such kindness and respect. When I checked in with my emotions, they told me that I was at ease in this man's presence, totally relaxed, and I had laughed more than I had in a long time. Our values seemed aligned regarding how we treat others and approached life. So far, so good! I was very content when he asked me out on a second date the following week, this time to a vegan restaurant. He had noted my dietary preferences and shown initiative, a big plus for me. Once again, I returned home feeling happy, hopeful and uplifted.

After two to three months of dating, we were both sure we wanted to only see each other. John (well, that's what I'll call him here) and I have been in a relationship ever since. I thank the dating app Gods every day that they facilitated our meeting. And, if I wasn't dating with my eyes opened, I may have missed him.

EXERCISE
Dating Journal Prompts

Below are some journal prompts to use after each and every date, to ensure your eyes remain wide-open, and you stay self-reflective, in control, and use your head as well as your heart when it comes to finding love.

What did you think of your date (the person)?

What did you think of the date itself?

Seeking Love

How did you feel in your body on the date, and what may this indicate to you?

Consider your relationship values, and how these matched up with your date.

Were there any big turns offs, values clashes, or boundary violations?

When Will It Happen For Me

Would you like to see this person again, and why or why not?

If you found these prompts helpful, you will enjoy my more detailed dating course, *Roadmap to Love*, which is all about finding a healthy partner in dating. The course includes a copy of *The Intuitive Dating Journal: The Ultimate Dating Companion For Empathic Women*, with further in depth prompts for self-reflection in dating. The self-paced course is all about more deeply understanding your relationship patterns and choices, identifying and steering clear of red flags, listening to your gut, and ultimately finding and choosing to be with a loving, emotionally available partner. You can find the course here: https://www.therelationshipspace.com.au/roadmap-to-love

CHAPTER TEN

How To Choose A Long-Term Partner

When I met my current partner, things felt completely different. I was a little perplexed and confused by his reliability and consistency in communication. The path was easier than it had ever been with anyone else. Easier, smoother, lighter, and surer. There wasn't an energy of fatigue, paralysing anxiety, or guessing games. It was another little lesson in listening to my feelings.

He asked curious questions on the apps, and this continued with text messages, and in real life. He showed me clear signs of interest from before the day we met and this hasn't ever changed. As our relationship progressed, his actions gave me the confidence to reach out more, feeling at ease that he would be happy to hear from me. There was true, uncomplicated reciprocity.

I used to complicate dating but, now I was learning, it could be surprisingly simple. It's interesting what happens, when you move out of the adrenaline of early dating and start to consider a person as a long-term partner. In a way, this is the trickiest bit of dating—the transition—when you're starting to look past the heady, early dates of excitement and consider: what would life be like with this human?

When Will It Happen For Me

I view your partner choice as your most critical life choice. It can determine your level of happiness for the rest of your life. It's a huge deal, and I want the very best for you—a solid and loving relationship that lasts the distance.

But here's the thing, I almost didn't meet my current partner. You see, just before I met him, I got all caught up in the intensity and chemistry I experienced with another man. A veritable Casanova, who was smart, suave, mature, and seemed like he wanted a real connection. It soon became illuminated that he was seeking a purely physical connection, perhaps with some conversation on the side. I can't believe I missed it! The truth is we all miss these things if we don't understand the power of our conditioning and attachment systems, and leave our guidebook behind. Once I realised what was happening, I was able to course correct, just in the nick of time. And then I went on a first date with my current partner ... who showed me how things should feel.

I really believe that the early stages of dating will be incredibly telling about a potential mate's capacity to offer you emotional warmth, empathy, connection, and reliability.

I've seen healthy, loving, securely functioning relationships change the lives of my clients, and being in one has radically changed my life for the better. A secure relationship is the base that allows you to go out into the world and navigate challenges, because no matter what happens you have a home and companion to return to. Besides journaling as your self-reflection weapon, there's more I want you to know. If you understand the principles in this chapter, you will be more likely to reach your goal of a safe relationship sanctuary with a partner.

This section of the book is all about checking in with the guidebook regularly, and using your head first, not merely your heart. As I was going through the emotions of dating, and looking for answers in how to do it with more wisdom, I delved into the world of red flags and emotional maturity. These two ideas were the anchors that steered me clear of relationship toxicity and into the arms of a healthy love. Let's unpack them together.

Red Flags, Green Flags

Most of us navigating the dating world aren't strangers to the concept of red flags. Red flags can be thought of as warning signs within another person that indicate the potential to hurt or cause harm. These external red flags can show up as uncomfortable or anxious feelings in our body. Green flags are the signs that tell us we can proceed safely and can expect things to go well.

Red flags are talked about by dating coaches and relationship experts all over social media. Many of my clients tell me they know how to spot them. And this is also true, however, something somewhere goes wrong. This is what I have observed tends to happen: we often don't end things in the early stages of dating when we spot a pesky little red flag. The unhealed part of us wants to hang in there a little bit longer, trying to find out how big or serious the red flag is, seeking to be sure that the red flag is in fact a red flag. We reconcile the red flag if we have in fact noticed it, and then we're deep into the relationship with heartfelt feelings involved and genuine care for the person we're with! And the further we're in, the bigger the feelings and longing to make it work.

What happens is, our 'urge to merge' tends to make us a little silly and sentimental, and prioritises keeping a connection rather than being rational and moving on. We're ruled by our emotions rather than reality. We tend to bend, compromise, and adjust our sense of what is a red flag. We minimise, downplay, and deny the severity of the red flag, and hyperfocus on all the good parts in our new person.

I certainly did this when I met my ex-partner. I downplayed his jealousy and insecurity and focused on how generous he was. If we have a background of trauma our sense of what red flags are is often skewed. The neglect we received from loved ones in the past has confused our sense of what treatment is unacceptable. Understanding what constitutes a relationship red flag is highly critical in helping you assess a potential partner's relational capacity.

As in the previous chapter, I urge you to tune in to your body. The presence of red flags in another can show up as agitation, restlessness, and anxiety in your nervous system. I think of one female client who was on constant eggshells in her relationship with a partner who was so easily triggered and found fault in everything she did and failed to accept any responsibility for his part in the dynamic. Big red flags.

Remember that the defining feature of a healthy relationship is one where security is co-created. Each partner is willing to self-reflect, listen, and do the work required to stay connected. I knew one of my client's was in a healthy relationship when she met a man with lots of green flags: he was in touch often, initiating and planning dates and eventually a holiday together. He was able to talk about their future, could share his feelings, and spoke openly of his past. And when they had their first disagreement, he listened to and took her feelings seriously. He did not withdraw for extended periods of time and was sure to let her know what he needed from her going forward. The biggest green flag was her nervous system was suddenly at ease. She wasn't free of anxiety

Seeking Love

and the new relationship did trigger her often, however, through communication and vulnerability, the couple bonded, and she felt more sure of being able to open up to him.

Here's my list of red flags (and you can certainly add your own). As you read, think about those that you have experienced previously:

- ♥ Overly sexual in their behaviour and failing to connect mentally or emotionally. This includes purely flirtatious or sexual texts and gestures, as well as a focus on sex being important to them in the beginning (this conversation is one that should evolve naturally with time, not be immediately present)
- ♥ Not prioritising actual, real dates where there's conversation and a shared activity; not initiating dates and you feeling like you're doing all the planning
- ♥ A significant lack of consistent communication, including silent treatment for several days on end
- ♥ 'Love bombing' including showering you with gifts or extravagant gestures and wanting to lock down a commitment quickly without truly getting to know you
- ♥ Lacking an ability to self-reflect. This may include not being able to share their part in relationship endings, or blaming others
- ♥ Lacking compassion for others and the human condition
- ♥ Being rude to others e.g. wait staff on dates, being irritable if you are a few minutes late
- ♥ A high value on money, image, status and aesthetics
- ♥ Having a narrow view of their family relationships; to view or categorise others as 'bad' can indicate a lack

of ability in emotional processing and recognising the complexity of the behaviour of others
- ♥ 'Trauma dumping' or oversharing traumatic details of their past, and you feeling like you're in the parent or therapist chair
- ♥ Quick to jealousy
- ♥ Being overly negative, pessimistic, and mistrusting of others
- ♥ A clear disregard for the rules of society
- ♥ A failure to show curiosity in you as a person
- ♥ They tell you about a history of a lack of commitment and are unsure about what they are looking for; it is okay if their interest for you grows and increases over time, but you should see and feel it growing clearly
- ♥ A disclosure of 'not being good in relationships' and a high emphasis on autonomy and independence. Again, this can shift with time and conversation, however, if it's not moving along, you need to reconsider

Think about the times you wished and hoped that they would commit if you just remained patient, or the times you were embarrassed by how they treated others. And also ask yourself how quickly these behaviours emerged. Often they were there at the beginning.

I really urge you to think deeply, listen to your feelings, and bring these red flags to a skilled therapist who can help you assess them more closely, so that you can make the wisest decision for you. The short-term pain of leaving a dead-end relationship will ease in time, and also open up space for a healthier dynamic.

Are Your Schemas Incompatible?

In Schema Therapy, there is something called 'Schema Chemistry' which means that we can experience intense emotions for someone that can potentially wound us, often because this emotional feeling is familiar and was experienced in the past. In other words, a present partner can activate childhood wounds, and the resonance is often described as 'it feels like I know you already'. Your younger, wounded self knows this feeling well, not the person; however, we often mistake this bodily sensation as 'chemistry' and a cue to proceed, rather than a cue to back away immediately. We are therefore not acting from our adult wisdom, but from our wounds.

I strongly suggest you watch out for feelings of intense attraction and chemistry with a partner. If you feel bursts of adrenaline, butterflies in your stomach, and feel like a school girl with an obsessive crush, I urge you to slow down. With Mr Casanova, I often felt out of my body. I wish I knew that my body was warning me rather than feeling convinced he was 'special'.

I'll outline some examples of schema chemistry here. In my own case, emotional deprivation schema predominated my worldview, and I often felt emotionally misunderstood. As such, I was drawn to partners who were low on empathy and emotional maturity, and were consumed by their own struggles. These partners tended to have schemas of defectiveness, insufficient self-control, and entitlement, and as such were unable to provide the emotional attunement that I longed for.

Schema chemistry helps explain why those of us with trauma can be drawn to those with narcissistic tendencies and entitlement. Their self-absorption, charm, and ability to put us on eggshells can activate our self-sacrifice, approval-seeking, and fear of abandonment all at once.

I have many female clients with approval-seeking and self-sacrifice schemas who focus on taking care of others in order to receive admiration, care and love. Unfortunately, they never receive the love they need, as they tend to attract partners who are withdrawn, cold, and unaffectionate. For much of the relationship these women are working overtime, giving love in the hope of receiving it. This pattern often started in childhood as a way to survive and continues across adulthood, until they recognise it.

A healthy love is not one that is earnt, but is freely given and received. As healthy adults, we want to prioritise a connection based on values and communication rather than intense physical and emotional chemistry. We want to feel calm in the presence of another, not in a state of activation. A healthy love will feel stable, grounded, and predictable.

Now let's turn to an equally important and related concept that I wish my younger self knew ten years ago.

Emotional Maturity Matters

One day my healing journey guided me to a wonderful and accidental discovery. At the end of 2021, in my hope to heal and find answers, I decided to enrol in The Holistic Psychologist's Self-Healers program. This program was valuable and included many of the principles from Schema Therapy and reparenting your inner child. It was in that program that I came across a book that changed my life, *Adult Children of Emotionally Immature Parents: How to Heal from Distant, Rejecting, Or Self-Involved Parents* by

Seeking Love

Lindsay C. Gibson. Gosh, that book was so validating, and also liberating.

I had spent years and years as a therapist talking to my clients about the building blocks of healthy relationships: empathy, warmth, validation, regulated emotions, perspective-taking, accountability, refraining from blame and defensiveness, and holding compassion for others. All these qualities tend to stem from a securely functioning individual with a healthy sense of self and a healthy trust in others. However, this was the first time I had seen this collection of traits defined as emotional maturity.

My second, earth-shattering realisation was that I had never dated a totally emotionally mature partner. Unfortunately, these traits of emotional immaturity in a partner contributed to ongoing conflict, as my feelings were invalidated, and I became more desperate and powerless to regulate my own emotions. It was a terrible relationship cycle.

My own journey in therapy had helped me identify my innate capacity for emotional maturity, as well as truly develop these skills further. We can all struggle with remaining emotionally mature when triggered so it is important we work at these skills. In doing so, you are more likely to find relationship happiness with a partner who is equally emotionally mature and committed to doing their part to cultivate secure ground for you both.

Within my current relationship with John, we both aim to bring emotional maturity to the table. I have never seen John lose his temper with me or resort to shaming or name-calling, and he has always remained calm and kind, even under pressure and within conflict. I have never witnessed him be demeaning or critical, even if he is frustrated. His compassion and ability to hold the other in mind is evident. Despite disagreements, which are infrequent, we hold on to our respect and care for each other, and continue to see the best in each other. Also, he never holds a grudge if I do become angry or upset. He is able to see those emotions as part of my humanity rather than a character flaw, and he reminds me that he loves 'grumpy Phoebe', that all my feelings are welcome and acceptable. This is also reciprocated; in that I do my best to hold in mind all the stress he is carrying and refrain from nagging and blaming. I have learnt to air any grievances immediately, and we work to a resolution, rather than allowing for tension and resentment to build up inside. Most of all, the therapy I have done has shown me that it is my responsibility to soothe myself when I am triggered, and that is not my partner's job. I can ask for comfort and empathy, but I must regulate my emotions first, take space if angry, and communicate my needs calmly. We remember that we are not mind-readers and must use our words if we need something from each other. It is this spirit of emotional maturity and self-responsibility that contributes to the health and stability of our relationship.

I urge you to cultivate emotional maturity in all your relationships. This means extending others compassion and accepting them for who they are. It means tolerating disagreement and not pushing for agreement, and not using punishment, withdrawal, emotional manipulation, guilt, or anger to control the actions of others. Emotional maturity is about simultaneously using the wisdom of our minds and the warmth of our hearts, and seeing both as valuable to human connection. I encourage you to read this book yourself to further equip you on your relationship path. Cultivating this skill is a gift to all your relationships.

Seeking Love

EXERCISE
Empowering Your Partnership Choice

Consider what we've covered in this chapter, and journal or take a few moments to think about the following questions:

What relationship red flags have you come across and want to remain on the lookout for?

_____
_____
_____
_____
_____
_____

Think about the traits of emotional maturity that you bring to your relationships and list them here.

_____
_____
_____
_____
_____
_____

When Will It Happen For Me

What traits of emotional maturity would you like to see in your (future) partner?

How would you like to feel in the presence of your partner?

CHAPTER ELEVEN

What Do You Want From Love?

I remember the moment I first felt loved by my current partner; the moment I knew with certainty that I was deeply cared for. It was a weekend like any other, filled with the usual chores, grocery shopping, and time with my sweet puppy. We were a few months into our relationship, and I was feeling more at ease than I ever had in a relationship before. From our first meeting, he had been funny, kind, and optimistic, and very responsive to my needs for connection. He was busy with work this weekend, as he often was. I had made it clear to him over those few months that I wanted a relationship built on time together, collecting memories, and sharing a vision for the future. However, things were still new, and I was still nervous about being too much or too needy for him. I'd still get little pangs of worry in my chest if I was wanting more and was going to have to ask for it.

This particular Sunday morning, one of the lights in my bathroom, a fluorescent tube, started flickering and zapping. I turned it off at the main switch and realised there was no way I could fix it myself. I started to notice the panic rise in my body, as the bathroom became pitch black and non-functional without it. I had few people to call on in these situations, and previous rejections when I needed help had cultivated an independent streak within me. These handy tasks are really not my strong point. I have always feared changing lights, as they feel like the ultimate, overwhelming, single girl's task that I just can't fit my head around. What type of bulb do I get, how bright, what should the fitting be, and how will I reach the high ceiling on my own without a ladder, which I would be scared to climb up anyway.

Thankfully, you can pay people to help you, so that's just what I did. Unfortunately, when my paid help arrived, my gut started to question him from the beginning. It just felt a bit 'off' but, yes, I let him into my apartment. I've discovered that one of the unfortunate legacies of trauma is that you can deny your own internal gut because you've been shown that your feelings don't matter (we'll talk more about this later).

I proceeded with the job because I was alone, desperate, and needing help. He was fake, overly charismatic, with exaggerated charm. Very quickly the situation unravelled, and I had an intimidating man in my apartment forcing work upon me that I did not require.

I was trying to remain cool, yet I was tense and felt like I was in a hostage negotiation. I was scared and stuck. I decided to text my partner to let him know what was happening. Of course, I tried to minimise the situation for fear of being a burden, but he read between the lines. Without me needing to prompt, he said he was hopping into an Uber immediately to be with me.

This was the day I became certain that this man, my new boyfriend, was truly a good one, capable of showing up for me, protecting me, and offering me love, nurturance and security.

Seeking Love

It wasn't a typical romantic gesture, yet it was deeply romantic, and it was just what I needed from a partner. It was like a big warm hug that said, 'I'm here for you no matter what. We're in this together.' This moment reassured me that he would run to my side and protect me when needed.

I felt loved and like I truly mattered. I didn't have to be self-sufficient, tough, and strong all the time. I could fall apart and that was okay, because he could catch me. His values of kindness, support, nurturing, and justice shone through that day. His values of teamwork, communication, and reciprocity are what I had been seeking and was grateful to have found.

What I've wanted from love has changed with age and wisdom, and I wonder whether this has changed for you too. I have come to care a lot more about my relationship values after the demise of my relationship with my last ex-partner. I had realised how much our values were misaligned and in conflict, and how strongly this had hindered my wellbeing.

When I was younger, I valued chemistry, attraction, depth, emotional intensity (red flag alert!), and someone showing interest in me. When I started dating again at thirty-six years old, I was looking for something else completely. This older, wiser, more mature me wanted a lot more from a potential partner and her relationship. I had a list and intended to approach any new relationships guided by my values. Values are so fundamental to who we are and what fulfills us, as was the case of my incredibly brave thirty-something year old female client who eventually decided within a few sessions that she had to leave her relationship. She felt so deeply in her soul that her purpose was to be a mother and to experience that journey with a partner, whereas her partner seemed hugely ambivalent. I always tell the women

I work with that they must go after what they truly long for. Why so?

Well, for a lot of the women I've seen and helped over the years, I have observed how we tend to approach love from a place of giving, rather than receiving, and from a place of uncertainty about how love should feel. We tend to seek relationships from a place of that old conditioning we spoke about here in these pages, from a blind spot that results in the same old pattern that ultimately fails us. I want you to do better, and you can. I want you to soar and set your sights on what you deeply long for.

Let's think about choosing love from a place of our heart's deepest desires, from our values. So, ask yourself: do you approach love from a place of what you want to receive, really? And is it time you opened your heart to really being cared for?

How Do You Feel Most Loved?

Love can take many forms and we all experience love in different ways. I see love as daily gestures of showing up for your partner. Dr Gary Chapman's Five Love Languages has been an incredibly helpful framework for myself and many of my clients when we consider love. Chapman describes that there are five ways that we each give and receive love: words of affirmation, quality time, receiving gifts, acts of service, and physical touch. We each feel loved in different ways, depending on our preference for each type of love.

The idea is, we can feel disconnected from our partner because we don't recognise how they're trying to show us love. And our partners can feel disconnected from us because we're

Seeking Love

not loving them in a way that matters to them. For instance, if your love language is physical touch, you might overlook, and underplay, your partner's gift of flowers, or that they left work early to go for a walk on the beach with you. In the same way, your partner might not value all the ways you vocally praise them, but they could crave a cuddle in bed—a love language that might not matter to you.

My love language has consistently been quality time, with some physical touch in the mix. I love spending uninterrupted time with my partner, preferably on a dinner date where we talk and share what's happening in our worlds. My partner's love language is acts of service, and he feels loved when I help him out with tasks that unburden him. He tends to give his love to me by working hard, so that our toy Cavoodle and I are provided for. Through my expression of love in ways that are less familiar to him, he has become more open to other forms of love including affection and gratitude. No wonder humans can struggle to feel loved by our partner when we feel loved and give love in such different ways.

What I suggest for female clients working with me is to embody love by giving that form of love to yourself. If you long for affirmation, give beautiful words of praise to yourself. And if you long for flowers, as Miley Cyrus reminds us in her hit song, you can buy those too. You filling up your own cup will benefit your partner. If you do have a partner, express with playfulness the type of love that you long to receive so that they know how best to show you love. You could cuddle up beside them in bed and say 'I really love it when you plan dinners for us and I get to get dressed up', or sneak up beside them, and with a kiss on the cheek say 'I feel so much lighter knowing you take care of the car for me'. Do this all with joy, gratitude and appreciation.

When Will It Happen For Me

So, how may this work in reality? Take a few moments to reflect upon the types of love you need and then visualise yourself receiving this love clearly from your partner, or a prospective partner in the future. Imagine the scene—your partner loving you in a way that fills your heart with comfort, pleasure and joy. How do you feel inside? How would you respond to them, if they loved you in that way, in that moment?

Now—because our partners are not mind-readers—think about how you can become more proactive in asking for the type of love you need. In fact, imagine that you were writing them a letter (or a text message you might actually want to send). How could you prompt them to notice the type of love that hits home for you?

Here are some scripts you could use:

Remember when you [ran a bath for me] the other night? That really made me happy. It's those small acts of kindness which make me feel really loved.

I can't stop thinking about our sex session last night. That was so hot—I loved it when you [insert memory].

I just wanted you to know, I'm wearing that [gift they gave you]. It really makes me feel loved when you buy little things, which you know make me happy.

It meant a lot to me that you left work early to spend time with me. Is there anything I can do to make you feel that loved?

You may also write what you would say to your partner if you were asking to receive a particular type of love. This is a mutual project, between you and your partner, not a way to test each other to see if they fulfill your requirements.

Over time, they may begin to share how they make others feel loved, or how their family shows love. And as your relationship progresses, look out for the ways in which your partner expresses love; it may be different to how you express love, but it is there.

One important step is to start by expressing appreciation and gratitude for the love that is there, and also express that you tend to feel loved in a different way. You're allowed to ask, and in fact, I encourage it. You're often making your partner's life so much easier by saying what you need, rather than having them guess. Trust that a loving partner wants to do what is necessary to make you feel loved. By knowing your values and communicating your desires, you increase your chances of getting exactly what you want. That sounds pretty good, doesn't it?

Values Are Your Guiding Star

It is quite common for me to meet couples with differing life values. Differences I have come across in my work are: desire to have children, how to raise children, financial goals, or where to live. The idea of separating is painful for couples like this, especially when there is so much love at stake. For one couple I've worked with, let's call them Liesel and Sam, they've ultimately decided not to have children, given that Sam doesn't feel strongly connected to the idea. For Liesel, this is devastating; however, she has been with Sam for many years and can't imagine a future without him. As a couple they find it hard to talk about the painful stuff and tend to avoid the big issues. My work with Liesel has been to help her grieve, and also connect with her nurturing and maternal instinct in other areas of her life. For Sam, my work with him has been to help him get more in touch with his emotions, so that he can show empathy for his partner. I have had to work with the couple to get them to each tap into their deeper emotions, tune into their bodies, and bring this into the therapy room, so that they become more connected to each other. Their values won't shift, however, their intimacy and level of support has.

Values are the guiding morals, ethics, standards and rules that you choose to live by; principles that are deeply important to you and integral to your very being. Our values define who we are and how we choose to live, a compass for our life's direction, including for love and relationships. I like to think of values as what matters most in my heart and what brings me a sense of peace and fulfilment.

My values give my life purpose and meaning amongst all the rough patches, a constant bright star that keeps me on the right path. I allow my values to define the essence of my spirit and my intention. By committing to acting by our values we remain noble and good. And in the face of obstacles or hardships, when life is filled with hurt and pain, you can look to your values to guide your choices. Despite the pain, there will be peace in your soul knowing that you stayed true to your values.

The first step is to get intimate with your own personal value system. If you don't know what your values are or need to clarify them further, use the exercises at the end of this chapter. For example, it matters hugely to me that I leave behind an impact on the world. My vision is to help women find a healthy love that empowers them in all they do in life; that they have a secure base to return to. I also knew better, this time, to search for a partner

Seeking Love

who shared similar values, as I believed this would bring depth and connection to the relationship.

Take a moment to consider how your values play into your personal relationships. What truly matters to you and what is the legacy that you want to leave behind? It can be bigger or smaller. Some things you may value include your family and being there for them, or travel and adventure, and experiencing different cultures and exposing yourself to different ideas and ways of life.

Now, think about the partner that you long to have in your life and the values they would possess. Consider how they would show up for others, what challenges they would pursue, the things that would give their life meaning, the very traits that they would radiate. Imagine how you would feel in the presence of a partner with an aligned set of values, who intimately knows themselves and what they stand for. I imagine you would feel more grounded and connected to a partner with such values as they act with integrity.

I turned to my values often when I was dating and reflected upon them as I dated. Knowing the values I longed for in a partner brought so much more intention, direction and clarity to dating. When I was unsure about the man I was dating or I was experiencing anxiety or unease, I'd pull out my journal, look at my relationship values and have a clearer direction. You can gauge the values of another quite early on in dating; it is evident in how they treat service staff, whether they arrive on time, in the way they talk about their previous relationships, family, and their life goals.

Here's some ways you can explore values through your relationship timeline:

Early Dating: bring it into conversation.

Don't be afraid to ask about your date's values and what truly matters to them early on, as they say a lot about a person. Your values don't need to perfectly align, but I believe there should be a high level of resonance, and respect for your values. As I touched on, I deeply regretted in my past relationships that I had compromised my value system in order to have a relationship. For example, one partner had so much shame around their own mental health and refused to engage in help. I strongly value help-seeking, self-responsibility and de-stigmatising mental health. No wonder we were clashing so terribly and our future felt bleak. There was little values alignment. Your values can protect you from a life of discontent.

As Dating Proceeds: Think big picture.

Begin to consider and assess a prospective partner's values for the bigger things in life. You are assessing both character and life direction values, and I want you to avoid the hurt of surprises. I meet many women who absolutely want children in their future. Some of them wouldn't mind if their prospective partner had children, others are open to adopting or fostering children, and others want to have their own child with their partner. Please consider this as it is so key for women, and I don't want you to compromise on this or anything that matters to you. If you are unsure about whether you do want children or not, and are approaching your mid-thirties, you may want to consider fertility options such as egg-freezing, as it can remove a lot of pressure. Other women prefer to leave it up to the universe so to speak. Life is short, and it's important you chase your dreams.

Seeking Love

Long-term Partnerships: Do a yearly audit.
Sit down together once a year (New Year's Day is a great time) and explore how your values, dreams and priorities are evolving. This is especially important after big milestones, like getting married, buying a house or becoming parents. Our values can evolve as we age, and it's not a deal-breaker for relationships, as long as you have open and transparent conversations, and attempt to step into your partner's shoes.

When I truly reflected on my values and chose to date men who seemed to match my values by observing their dating profiles and our initial conversations, things really begun to shift for me. I seemed to draw in more men who equally valued education and self-learning, that were also looking for love and connection, valued their physical and emotional health, loved travel and adventure, and had more qualities of resilience. Overall, it seemed I met more dates who had lives that they enjoyed and felt proud of, and were more secure in themselves. It was a positive experience for me.

I was also more empowered and able to identify the dates who didn't align well with me, and let go with ease. You can start dating guided closely by your values and begin to witness how things evolve quickly. I'm sure you have intended to date guided by your values, however, I wonder how much you have compromised on these. I know I have compromised many times before. This time you can do it a little more deliberately by constantly referring back to your values and the vision of life that you have written down for yourself.

EXERCISE
Love Me, Love My Values

Consider what we've covered in this chapter, and take a few moments to think about the following:

Write your values here, focusing on your top three to five values for your current or future relationship. Write why they matter so deeply to you.

Feel free to take from some of my values below, or come up with your own: *Authenticity, Adventure, Courage, Connection, Delight, Encouragement, Fun, Financial Security, Hardworking, Intelligence, Loyalty, Optimism, Playfulness, Perseverance, Resilience, Spontaneity, Travel, Vitality, Zest.*

CHAPTER TWELVE
Letting Love In

At this point—about four months into dating my new partner—I was feeling pretty pleased with myself. The work had paid off: I had brought clear intentionality to seeking a mate; I'd thoroughly considered the type of partner I truly longed for, the character traits and values he would possess; I knew the values I wanted our relationship to be defined by; and I was clearer on how I wanted love to feel this time around.

If one of my clients had come and told me they'd come to this point in a session, I would have given them a high-five. 'See, look how far you've come! Doesn't this relationship feel secure and sustainable?' I felt confident and optimistic. I had met a great partner and now, surely, love would proceed on a beautifully smooth course into the future.

So, you can imagine my rude shock and surprise when, out of nowhere, my new partner 'let me down'. You see, from the beginning, John had generally sent me a text message each morning to see how I was and wish me a good day. My nervous system felt at ease and reassured. And then, one day... the message didn't arrive!

When Will It Happen For Me

As time to head to work approached and I still hadn't heard from him, my panic rose. I remember my heart sinking and my gut tensing, as I walked the short walk to my office, filled with anxiety and doom about what it all meant, followed by surges of anger that he would 'do that to me'. This was then followed by persistent ruminations of whether I should reach out to him first or not, and what it would mean if I did text first. Would I seem too needy? Would he even reply? Did I in fact matter to him?

My seemingly ideal partner had hurt me, and I spiralled. And to be frank, I didn't cope well with this at all. I suddenly found myself closing off to love, pulling away from it and him, risking sabotaging it all, despite so deeply longing for love and connection. And I nearly didn't realise it.

I knew what I would say to a client who came to me in this quandary. I would tell them with kindness that their emotional reaction is pointing to an inner child wound being activated, and perhaps their feelings in this moment are more tied to the past than the present. That I do understand their longing for love and closeness, and in particular, a reliable and stable presence. However, I would also remind them that their partner is a human being with their own stressors, and is going to let them down sometimes, and that is okay. It happens, even in the closest partnerships. I'd remind them to focus on the overall pattern of their relationship, and remind them of the general consistency that their partner has offered so far.

But all my professional knowledge didn't help me in that moment. My anxiety and accompanying self-protection took hold of me in ways that challenged us both. I started to internally fester, to blame John, and to question if he had what it took to be a good partner.

Seeking Love

It wasn't just this one incident, either. Over the next six months, this would happen any time that I perceived or felt that John had let me down. I say 'perceived' as, in reality, he was warm, communicative and caring. Yet, I couldn't stop these intense waves of emotion. I would stew over how busy he was at times and become frustrated when he didn't text in a regular pattern or prioritised his work. I would hold on to my frustrations, withdraw from him, and put my phone on mute. I confess, part of me wanted to punish him with my silence. And my silence meant I wasn't saying how I felt, or what I needed, and he was clueless as to my triggers.

Thankfully, not all was lost. This is where working with a therapist in the first throws of a new relationship is so useful. Because your new partner may be too polite to call you out on your shit—luckily my astute schema therapist was happy to do so. In one coaching session, she said to me: 'you know, you actually can tell your partner how you feel, that's what adults do in healthy relationships. You can guide him in getting to know you and what you need. Just do it in a soft and gentle way.' It sounds simple now, but it floored me back then.

What dawned on me, within a flash, was how much I was responsible for our disconnection: I had to stop sabotaging this relationship by keeping my feelings and triggers inside. It was me, not him, who was failing to let love in. I was doing a terrible job of sharing my inner world with John and, if I wanted this relationship to work, I was going to have to find a way to let love in.

The problem is, I had so many fears around being seen for all that I am. Would he really love me if he knew all my hang-ups? Don't people want a partner who is easy and breezy? Could another human being really deal with all my insecurities and needs? Would he have the compassion and patience required to understand my fears and be prepared to meet me halfway?

To find out, I had to drop my defences and open up, which brings us to the magic word—vulnerability. But, before we understand true vulnerability, let's delve in a little deeper into how we get in our own way, and block love (sometimes in a way that becomes a deal breaker).

How We Block Love

I have observed countless clients block love and shut it out when they are hurting and fearful. Sadly, many female clients who have come to me never make it on a date as they're worried about failing at dating and choose avoidance instead. I try to remind them what this move is costing them, and that love doesn't come to those who wait—it comes to those who date!

And then I think of other clients who struggle, like me, once they're in a steady relationship. I had one client who, in arguments with her partner, failed to hear and acknowledge his attempts to make amends, and instead went on endless tirades about how hurt she had been. Her paralysing fear turned into stony anger that ended up pushing her partner away. Through her wall of hurt and anger, she was unable to receive his attempts to show love and make amends. It truly saddened me to witness. I don't want you to end up in such a sad and hopeless place.

I can also think of countless, beautiful clients who have chosen partners that aren't emotionally ready, available, willing, or able to love them. This is another form of blocking yourself from being loved fully and completely by another who is able to give you the

Seeking Love

love and presence you long to receive. A diluted version of love isn't really love, and can do you more harm than good.

Despite the truth that so many of us long to find love, we often subconsciously put up walls to block love because quite simply, we're terrified of getting hurt. Many of us have never witnessed a healthy love and have experienced rejection when at our most fragile, emotional, or needy, whether as a child or in past romantic relationships. Given this, it takes huge amounts of courage, trust, and vulnerability to let love in. Sometimes the familiar path of blocking love feels like a safer option.

Let's take a specific look at ways in which you may be blocking love across the cycle of dating to being in a relationship.

Contemplating Dating & The Early Stages

See if you can identify yourself in any of the behaviours below that block love, noting that they tend to be driven by fear:

- ♥ Pretending or lying to oneself by denying that you want love.
- ♥ Throwing oneself into everything else but dating, including work and hobbies.
- ♥ Not showing up with authenticity and vulnerability on dating apps, or active avoidance of dating altogether.
- ♥ Not prioritising dating by not replying to messages, or nit-picking the quality or frequency of the messages received.
- ♥ Playing 'hard to get' or being unresponsive when a partner reaches out for connection.
- ♥ Not reaching out at all once the relationship is more established.

When Will It Happen For Me

Settling When It Comes To Love

See if you can identify yourself in any of the behaviours below that block love, noting that they tend to be driven by fear:

- ♥ Staying in undefined relationships for lengthy periods of time, and failing to seek clarity about the direction or definition of the relationship.
- ♥ Dating a partner with unfinished relationship business, for example, still living with their ex.
- ♥ Staying too long in unfulfilling relationships, including with an emotionally unavailable partner.
- ♥ Ignoring your 'gut' and the nagging feeling that something feels 'off'.

Within A Relationship:

See if you can identify yourself in any of the behaviours below that block love, noting that they tend to be driven by fear:

- ♥ Shutting down or withdrawing from the relationship.
- ♥ Denying or minimising ones emotional needs altogether.
- ♥ Failing to express what you need or saying you're 'fine' when that's far from the truth.
- ♥ Focusing on trying to fix the relationship by bringing up every small issue.
- ♥ Focusing on trying to change your partner and their flaws, through anger, criticising, blaming, or other means.
- ♥ Having very high expectations of your partner.
- ♥ Failing to soothe your own anxiety within the relationship and leaning on your partner too heavily.

Seeking Love

I wonder how many of these behaviours stood out to you, resulting in you ultimately blocking love from your life. As hard as it can be to face yourself, note whether you can take responsibility for your part in blocking love, rather than blaming dates or a new partner.

As this list shows, in all stages of a relationship (and even before one begins), we can push love away without meaning to. Self-protection mode can kick in as soon as we perceive a relationship threat, resulting in our walls going up, or anger and frustration surfacing to hide our vulnerability.

I want to assure you that, if you relate to these feelings and behaviours, it can and does get easier. Sometimes, however, it involves looking back (way back!) to where you learnt to protect yourself in this way in the first place—and why you find letting people in so damn scary.

Vulnerability Is The Only Way

These days 'vulnerability'—the willingness to show emotion, or to allow one's weaknesses to be seen and known—has become a buzzword. But it's for good reason. In relationships, whether they are romantic or otherwise, vulnerability is the glue that builds strong bonds, and helps us to weather the storms of challenges.

Vulnerability means a commitment to sharing your inner world with your partner on a regular basis, so they come to understand you. You want to help your partner to develop an ongoing template of you, so that your emotional world makes sense to them.

So, there are two key gifts that vulnerability can provide. The first is that if you are truly vulnerable, you will experience being loved for who you are. When you reveal your humanity, needs, emotions and wounds to your partner, they get to experience the real you. Vulnerability allows you to be seen, accepted and loved for who you truly are—an imperfect human being. To me this is the greatest gift one could ever experience.

The second gift that vulnerability provides is that of connection. Time and time again, in my therapy office, I witness what happens when someone is vulnerable in couples therapy. A partner is moved by their beloved's vulnerable disclosure. Tears well up in their eyes and more compassion and warmth is experienced which bonds a couple further. The partner sharing their feelings feels seen and accepted. If we can reframe vulnerability as the bridge the connects two lovers, vulnerability becomes your relational superpower, rather than something to be feared by either of you.

Below are some ways that vulnerability can be practised in your relationship (and this is a practice, not a one-and-done event). Being vulnerable is an ongoing commitment that, at certain times, can feel easier than others:

- ♥ The real you is exposed. You stop being angry or withdrawn, and you begin to show the softness, humanity, and raw emotions that are behind the mask. Vulnerability means sharing your past wounds with your partner in a gentle way that allows them to understand you more fully.
- ♥ You share your struggles as well as your triumphs with your partner.
- ♥ You share your fears, worries and anxiety about the relationship with calm and non-blaming language.

Seeking Love

- ♥ You share some stories from your childhood, or moments that were particularly upsetting from your previous relationships.
- ♥ You share your present feelings, and you may link them back to past life experiences that reveal the story of why you have been triggered now.
- ♥ You talk with self-responsibility and ownership. A vulnerable disclosure around anxiety may sound like *'I just wanted to share a little bit of my past with you to help you understand why I get anxious when I feel there's distance between us'*. Or, if you're feeling hurt by a partner's actions, a gentle *'I do feel quite anxious when we fight, it makes me worry things aren't okay between us'*. You are owning the part you play in a situation, and how your perception of events is impacting your reactions.

Vulnerability is not:

- ♥ 'Trauma-dumping' or simply venting about all of your past hurts to your partner without awareness of the impact of this on them. It is a lot more intentional than that: expressing what is likely to trigger you, how you feel inside, and what you may need from your partner, whether listening, patience, understanding, or compassion.
- ♥ Spoken in anger. As I have alluded to, anger and frustration are not vulnerable emotions, and I have never seen them result in eliciting care from a partner. In fact, anger will likely overwhelm them and push them away. The key is to allow the anger to melt and soften, and discover what's happening underneath those feelings,

and then communicate that. What you'll likely find is fear of rejection, abandonment, loss, or failure.
- ♥ Finger-pointing or blaming. In dating, a 'vulnerable disclosure' could be framed positively, rather than as a complaint. For example, telling your partner, *'I really look forward to hearing from you'*, or *'I really like where this is heading'*, or *'I feel really safe and reassured when you check-in with me'*.

Vulnerability and Your Schemas

Coming back to Schema Therapy, exploring our limiting beliefs can help us to understand why we feel unsafe to be vulnerable. Consider the schemas you identified with in our earlier chapters. How could they be stopping you from letting your partner—or future partners—really know you?

Fear of Abandonment

Remember, if you have a fear of abandonment schema, you are likely to believe you will be left. With vulnerability, you may worry that, if you present a full picture of who you are, it will give your partner a reason to leave you, or to choose someone else over you.

> **Antidote:** Remind yourself, that vulnerability brings closeness, because you show the real you. When partners share emotions, they're building a more secure attachment between them.

Seeking Love

Defectiveness and Shame
If you have a defectiveness schema, you are likely to believe you are worthless. With vulnerability, you may believe that your emotions make you weak, needy and a bad partner.

> **Antidote:** Remind yourself, that your vulnerability makes you human. Also remind yourself that younger you probably needed more acceptance and understanding when she was feeling big emotions. You can now choose compassion instead.

Emotional Deprivation
If you have an emotional deprivation schema, you are likely to believe that no one can truly nurture you and understand your feelings. With vulnerability, you may hold back because you fear your partner won't be able to show empathy and care.

> **Antidote:** Remind yourself, that your vulnerability is now welcome. You can be the one to validate your own emotions, and that if you want to break this belief, you're going to have to risk sharing. Be fair with what you expect of your partner, and offer them gentle guidance too.

Self-Sacrifice
If you have a self-sacrifice schema, you are likely to believe that your emotional struggles take the back-seat to those of others. With vulnerability, you may find yourself being the support and listener to others, and not allow yourself to receive that.

> **Antidote:** Remind yourself, that your vulnerability and emotional needs are equally important. Remember that those that truly care want to be there for you, so try and give them a chance to support you by opening up.

Emotional Inhibition

If you have an emotional inhibition schema, you are likely to view emotions as weak and uncomfortable. With vulnerability, you may find yourself doing all you can to not feel.

> **Antidote:** Remind yourself, that you have capacity to stretch yourself and begin feeling. Start by increasing your emotional vocabulary, and linking these feeling words to your experiences.

Of course, there are other schemas that can block our vulnerability. Use these examples as a starting point to trigger your own vulnerability, whatever your schemas may be.

It may be very hard for those of you who are anxious to trust in the magic of vulnerable self-disclosure, tapping into your fear of being too needy. We will work further on those worries in the next section of the book. However, for now, can you trust that in a loving relationship, your feelings matter? I was fortunate enough to witness the most incredible relationship transformation between my female client and her husband over the course of her attendance of my women's group. She got really brave by sharing her triggers and inner world, and he begun to respond in turn. Their compassion, empathy and new insights allowed their connection to flourish once again.

So, what happened in my relationship? As I shared my inner

Seeking Love

world more and more, John expressed gratitude for sharing my feelings with him and said my transparency made it easier for him to share his feelings too—he actually liked this vulnerable part of me a lot.

Often one partner's vulnerability prompts the other's vulnerability, building more depth and connection over time. It's also important not to panic if your partner seems overwhelmed by your disclosures or less open than you; their pace may be different to yours and that is okay. Sit back and observe the trajectory of vulnerability as the relationship progresses—and if you are uncertain, seek the advice of a trusted therapist.

EXERCISE
Vulnerable Communication Prompts

To help you on your journey of letting love in, here is a great exercise to improve your vulnerability.

Have a go at expressing a feeling and need vulnerably by completing the following:

I tend to feel really anxious when _____ _____

(name trigger e.g. distance, communication breakdown) and

I start to worry about _____ _____ *(name the relationship worry).*

This feeling of _____ *(name emotion) is related to a past experience when* _____ _____

(share the origin of the trigger), and

I'd really like it if _____ _____

(express relationship need e.g. a future plan, a text message check-in, a conversation).

PART FOUR

Building Security In Love

CHAPTER THIRTEEN
Being A Grown Up In Love

We talked in earlier chapters about how our inner child can hold us back and sabotage our relationships. Well, it's never more apparent than when you're moving from the honeymoon period into a more settled and secure relationship. You've moved out of the throws of passion when your life was full of novelty and abundant messages filled with compliments. Now you're moving into a more steady rhythm of a shared together—and your inner child is missing the attention!

In Schema Therapy, one of the modes, or parts of ourselves that is present in each of us to varying degrees is the 'healthy adult'. When I work with any client, my goal is to help them bring as much of their 'healthy adult self' to their relationship as possible. If they can achieve that, their relationship has a much better chance of weathering any storm and lasting. What does that mean? As you engage with your evolving relationship, you do it with the safety and security of your adult self; you take responsibility for your emotions, and you try to limit the moments when you are triggered by your schemas (fear of abandonment, failure, emotional deprivation etc—turn back to pages 65–66 for a reminder).

As my relationship with John evolved, it became very obvious when my inner child took the reins. I would be easily triggered, needy, and my emotional reactions felt overwhelming and out of proportion. My fears and worries would come out as frustration and anger.

I vividly remember getting ready for a gathering where I was going to meet some of John's friends for the first time. I was going to meet John there and asked him to text me when he was leaving his place to plan my arrival timing, as I didn't want to be there alone and not know anyone too well.

I recall being in the bathroom, attempting to curl my hair, and feeling unsettled and shaky. I couldn't really focus on my hair, as I worrying about what to wear, and how it would all go. John is a social, bubbly guy who loves his friends dearly, and I was feeling the pressure of the day, knowing that I was the first partner he'd introduced to friends before. John is also often in the moment, spontaneous and very easy going; I am a deep-thinker, planner, and organiser, and care probably too much about what others think of me. Anyway, John forgot to text me on his way to the party, which resulted in some anxiety and frustration on my part.

Once I got to the party, he seemed less engaged with me, and at some point, got caught up in a conversation with another woman who was on her own at the party. This brooding, fiery agitation arose inside of me, and I felt I needed to get out of there. I'd done my best to engage in other conversations with his friends, but felt I didn't have more to give. There was still an ache inside.

As I said goodbye to John that afternoon, I exchanged some quick, heated words. I didn't really understand where all that hurt came from in that moment. It wasn't until much later, once I had replayed the event in my mind, that I processed what had happened. I had felt totally abandoned and rejected by him. My inner child wounds of abandonment had caused me to overreact and lash out at him.

I also didn't want to keep being the type of girlfriend who is triggered by her partner's behaviours and live in anxiety and discontent forever. In order to heal these wounds, I had to go back in time, to where these feelings had started. This isn't about blame—a wounded inner child will never heal through judgement and shame. It's about getting curious and understanding your inner child better. It's about introducing your healthy adult so that 'they' and your inner child can actually work together.

Bringing in Adult Supervision

If you've just learnt that you've been at the whim of your inner child in your intimate relationships, it can be quite a rude awakening! A stark realisation that you may not always be bringing the best of you, your healthy adult self, to your relationships. The good news is, in seeing, understanding, and connecting with your inner child, you are now accessing the healthy adult part of you too. The healthy adult part of you does the caring role, supporting the inner child and, in turn, your healing.

Let's unpack what it means to be a healthy adult, and I'll guide you in how you can access that part of you more and more.

Being A Healthy Adult

The ultimate goal of Schema Therapy may be considered to have as much access as possible to our healthy adult. If our inner child part settles down and is soothed, we are more able to access our healthy adult. It is the healthy adult part of us that does the soothing in the first place.

In the midst of overwhelming, raw, child-like emotions, there are times when a more grounded, wise, knowing part of us takes over to offer calm and reassurance. That is your healthy adult.

A healthy adult is an individual who is able to access and see the value of both rational thought and emotions, and uses both to guide their life. A healthy adult has a strongly developed sense of empathy and compassion that is directed towards the self and others. A healthy adult is able to hold perspective and not lose touch of reality; they can trust in the goodness of life, and get back to a sense of calm because they know that in the end, everything is going to be okay. And this trust comes from backing themselves and believing in their capacity to manage whatever comes their way.

This doesn't mean that a healthy adult doesn't fall apart or feel overwhelmed by life every now and then—in fact, they expect this to happen because they accept their humanity and vulnerability. They're just able to access their inner strength, resources and coping skills to get through life. This maps on to the concept of emotional maturity that we touched on earlier when evaluating dating choices. I strongly believe that like attracts like and being a healthy adult increases your chance of being in relationship with another healthy adult.

Here are some traits and hallmarks of a healthy adult that I believe you should keep cultivating for relationship satisfaction:

Building Security In Love

- **Having healthy boundaries:** Boundaries are the limits we define regarding what behaviours we will and won't tolerate in our lives. A healthy adult knows their limits and has clear boundaries and expectations about the behaviour of others. A healthy adult will feel able to say 'no' without guilt or shame and value their emotional wellbeing above others, whilst remaining compassionate towards others.
- **Listening to themselves and their needs:** This concept is a requirement for boundaries. Having a strong connection to self and your emotional world allows a healthy adult to define their emotional, physical, mental, and energetic needs.
- **Knowing what makes you happy:** Having a strong inner sense of what fulfills you whether work, hobbies, friendships, intellectual stimulation, creativity, and play, and getting those needs met.
- **Self-validation:** A healthy adult is able to validate their own emotional world by assessing what emotions are coming up for them in a given moment, and offering some validating words.
- **Self-compassion:** A healthy adult attempts to not engage in shame, blame, or criticism of self, and believes that kindness goes further in creating change in life.
- **Self-discipline:** A healthy adult works on emotion regulation, planning, goal-setting and creating a routine for themselves to get the best out of life. They know when it's time to rest and when it's time to urge themselves on.
- **Accepts others as they are:** A healthy adult is at ease with individual differences and accepts others as they are, and doesn't feel the need to change others.

- ♥ **Self-acceptance:** A healthy adult sees the best in themselves, is able to identify their own strengths, and offers encouragement and praise to themselves. They equally accept their flaws with kindness and are comfortable with self-development if necessary.
- ♥ **Self-reflection:** A healthy adult is able to turn inwards and assess their strengths and flaws with warmth and honesty and does not shy away from their internal world, but sees it as a source of information.

In essence, I believe that a healthy adult does the work needed to be the best human they can be because their healing and well-being matters to them. They also do the healing work because they don't want their wounds to negatively impact others. And with that, here's one final lesson about being a healthy adult that I want everyone to know and embrace.

You're Responsible For You

Many of us seek relationships for what they can offer us: support, empathy, connection, comfort, companionship, stability. And seeking that in another is understandable, they're human needs. I just often see disaster when we place the responsibility on our partner to be a constant source of those things.

Now, if you feel quite disappointed by me telling you that you're responsible for getting your own needs met in a relationship, I was there once too. If you feel intensely hurt, sad, or enraged by this statement, it likely points to an unhealed inner child wound. Or maybe you're still processing the whole idea of self-responsibility and are a little confused by it; you may find yourself thinking ... well isn't the role of a partner to listen, show empathy, validate my emotions, and be attentive to my needs?

Yes, a partner can do that, but I suggest you don't expect that of them on a regular basis if you're longing for an ongoing happy, healthy, dynamic.

My philosophy of self-responsibility was formed by my own healing journey, and what I was witnessing in my therapy sessions with clients. In the past, my deficits in emotional self-soothing had contributed to sending me into the depths of relationship despair. My relationship with John felt like smooth sailing compared to past relationships, and I knew it was because I was growing in my self-soothing capacity. Professionally, there were lessons I had observed too.

A core component of couples therapy is teaching individuals to offer validation and support to each other. Yet, this approach didn't always work, and it felt to me that something was amiss. In what I could see, this strategy was only minimally effective because it failed to take into consideration the need to heal the inner wounds of the individual that were being triggered within the relationship. We must heal ourselves first—then we're less at risk of being triggered by our partner's words or actions.

Let me ask you to suppose what happens if you're in a relationship where you're not getting a lot of empathy? Perhaps your partner is stressed, overwhelmed or preoccupied for a long period of time or lacks the emotional skills to support you. And what if you become overly focused and reliant on your partner to understand your every emotion and validate it? Quite honestly, your partner is not a parent or superhero, and the pressure you can put on them by seeking this, could contribute to making things worse.

When Will It Happen For Me

That's why I deeply encourage each and every individual I see to work on 'self-responsibility'.

I define self-responsibility as a focus on going inwards first when you are triggered within your relationship, rather than focusing outwards. That is, the validation can come from within, rather than from another. I'm not saying to never seek support from another; you're human and need connection. However, simply observe what happens in your life when you apply the powerful skill of self-soothing first, and then seek connection from others afterwards. Your emotions will be more processed and softened, and you'll be clearer on what support you need from another. You may even find you don't need another's validation, yet to receive it would be a lovely bonus.

Here are the steps to apply to bring self-responsibility into your life:

1. As soon as you notice you are triggered and feeling an emotional response, stop, slow down, and observe what is happening inside of you.
2. Name any emotions, thoughts, and physical sensations.
3. Ask yourself what you need right now? Think of the core needs we have touched on previously: reassurance, validation, empathy, encouragement, hope.
4. See if you can offer some kind, compassionate, wise words to yourself right now.
5. Remind yourself that it is up to you to get your needs met.
6. Check in and see how things are feeling. Perhaps that's all you needed. And if you need to share something with your partner, that's okay too.

Building Security In Love

I'll always remember the first moment, in one of our repetitive arguments, when I didn't let my inner child react to John; when I didn't look to him for reassurance and validation. Instead, I called in my healthy adult self to soothe myself, comfort myself, and remind myself that I was safe and loved—whether he was in my life, or our relationship ended.

This is the magic of connecting with your healthy adult self. Yes, it helps to smooth over bumps in your relationship. But it also offers a part of you—an inner relationship—that will always be there, until your dying breath. In the future, whether you're single, coupled or anywhere in between, you can access the healthy adult—and that's an incredible comfort!

EXERCISE
A Healthy, Healed Me

Take a moment to consider these questions, either by writing them down in a journal or just taking a moment to contemplate the answers:

What are your own personal thoughts, feelings, and behaviours that indicate you're accessing your healthy adult?

What core traits of a healthy adult do you currently possess, and what traits would you like to cultivate more of?

Building Security In Love

How will the philosophy of self-responsibility shift your relationships?

CHAPTER FOURTEEN
The Hiccups of Healing

I take a lot of comfort and reassurance from the knowledge that all couples fight, even the closest ones. Healthy couples don't fear fighting and view it as part and parcel of partnership. What matters is how they move through and repair after the conflict. I was, and still am, learning this truth in my own relationship.

It was about six months into our relationship, and John and I were happy and growing in closeness. In fact, a dream of mine was about to come true. For as long as I can remember, I had longed to travel overseas with a partner and share an adventure with them. It was the epitome of couples goals for me. Travel lights me up inside and I am at my best when I am exploring a foreign place, absorbing its culture, cuisine and sights, and getting lost in the moment. So, you can imagine my elation when John asked me to accompany him to his friends' destination wedding, to be held in two countries, India and The Maldives. I was so happy; I almost couldn't fathom what he had asked me.

In the November, I met John at the airport, filled with excitement for our first overseas adventure together. It felt like such a significant relationship step, being invited into his life and friendship circle even more than I had been before. What made this trip even more incredible was that, when I arrived at the airport, I discovered that John had upgraded us to business class. He has always been hardworking and generous, but I was shocked by this incredible gesture. I was caught so off guard that I initially thought the woman at the check-in counter had made an error when she presented us with our boarding passes.

Everything that transpired on the trip was incredible—we laughed, danced, ate like royalty, and swam in the crystal waters below our overwater bungalow. My relationship was truly bringing me so much joy and I felt so blessed. I truly felt special, prioritised, and cared for in a way that I'd never felt before. I got to spend these glorious days with my new best friend. Of course, the holiday had to end, and I was going to miss John as I settled back into reality.

A week later, we flew home together, tiredly collected our luggage from the carousel, and walked out to the taxi rank, due to part ways and travel back to our separate homes. We waited together in line and John got into his taxi first, and then off he went. There was no warm embrace goodbye, just what felt to me like a casual farewell. And, in that moment, anger and hurt washed over me in seconds, at a speed quicker than my taxi pulling in.

What I later learnt was that John rode home happily and oblivious to my hurt. Two individuals with different relationship histories and triggers experienced this one event so very differently. And how ironic it was that this 'relationship hiccup' would transpire at a time when we had just spent a magical time together. Why did this have to happen?

As a relationship therapist, it's clear to me. But, as a human, in that moment, I couldn't see it with such clarity. My inner child had re-emerged, feeling rejected and abandoned when John departed from the airport taxi rank; our post-holiday bliss quickly dissolving into post-holiday blues. One moment you can feel so loved and secure in your relationship, and then hit these rocky moments, almost out of nowhere. Your partner's actions unintentionally cause pain, and you lose sight of their perspective and good intentions.

Fortunately, we were able to navigate our way back to connection. Couples can do this when they care about each other and are open to hearing each other's feelings and perspectives. The next day, I was honest with John about how triggered I felt during our goodbye, and he was quick to reassure me that I was mistaken. He'd had an amazing time with me, and he'd gone home feeling excited about our future. He also said, he was sorry that I had felt that way and that he was glad that I'd been able to be so honest with him.

To repair, each partner must be willing to admit their part in the conflict and work towards restoring connection because they care about each other. If you want to have a healthy relationship, you must commit to practicing the art of relationship repair—and that's what we're going to talk about in this chapter.

Repairing The Bond

A couple's bond is sacred, and I suggest you treat it as such. Your partner is now your primary attachment figure and can be your biggest source of safety and comfort, if you work at providing that to them also. There are times when your couple bond can feel steadfast and, at other times, insecure, when one or both partners are sitting with unresolved hurt.

A couple's bond or attachment is impacted by what therapists call 'relationship ruptures'. A rupture is a relationship injury that can be small or severe; for example, from forgetting an important reminder to a betrayal such as an affair. Ruptures can be infrequent or numerous, insidious or obviously painful.

I once spoke about relationship ruptures in a piece for the Australian online publication, *Mamamia*. In that article, the journalist, Isabella Ross, described relationship ruptures as 'papercuts'. The description is quite fitting. Seemingly small relationship wounds, such as being dismissed, ignored, unappreciated, and criticised, are repeated over and over across the course of the relationship, and when ignored can cause relationship death. Yes, it can be that dramatic.

It's not an exaggeration to say that every relationship papercut needs emotional first aid. The offender must repair the wound. Wounds can heal when the wounded party feels seen, understood, validated and acknowledged. Accountability and apology are critical for relationship repair. Relationship repair is essential for the ongoing health of all relationships.

The Art of Relationship Repair

Here's a common pattern of relationship destruction that I often see in my practice, and how it can be healed. In many of the couples I work with, one partner's criticism begins to wear the other down. The criticised partner begins to feel at a loss, as if they are never enough for their partner and their self-esteem takes a big hit. To repair, a sincere, heartfelt recognition and apology is needed that contains the following essential ingredients:

Building Security In Love

- ♥ Recognition and behaviour change: Ideally, the critical partner catches themselves in action and stops their criticism
- ♥ An acknowledgment of the emotional impact on their partner. For example: *"I know I was using critical language, and how upsetting that can be because it makes you feel so unloved"*
- ♥ An apology: *"I'm sorry for my actions and how much it hurts. I'm going to work on managing my emotions better, so you don't feel that way"*

This apology must remain free of defensiveness, including justifying, explaining, or minimising their actions. This will only diffuse the sincerity of the apology. Whether you meant to hurt your partner or not, their feelings are valid and what you must apologise for is the hurt inflicted. A healthy adult apologises because your partner and the relationship matters to you more than being right. If you don't learn to repair, every relationship you are in is at risk of failing. Whilst repair does wonders, behaviour change is critical. Criticism, a lack of appreciation, defensiveness, silent treatment, and other wounding behaviours must vanish in order for trust to be restored.

This is why the repair between John and I, after that incident, was effective. First of all, I tried to soothe my anger, and figure out what may have been going on for him. I knew I'd only find out if we talked, but I waited until my emotions had settled before I brought up my feelings with him, because I didn't want to be reactive and to lack clarity. I was able to share how I had been feeling, and he listened. Listening to John share his own perspective and reaction to my initial anger was also illuminating. It was then that I witnessed his inner wounds being revealed to me. We must remember that our partner has their own wounds too.

Meet Your Partner's Inner Child

All human beings have wounding and, just as you have an inner child, your partner does too. Their inner child part may panic in relationship conflict, fear rejection, or feel not good enough in some way. This concept has often sobered me when we fight, and I see it connect couples when I work with them. Helping partners recognise each other's inner child wounds has become a core part of how I do couples therapy. Couples are more able to repair in the present when they understand the impact of the past on their partner. Conflict is more complicated than the present moment, it is often the meeting of two inner children, both longing to feel loved and accepted.

When I told John I was upset about the airport farewell, he was able to share that he was hurt. My anger made him feel as if I wasn't grateful for all he had done for the holiday. It made him feel like his love wasn't enough. This beautiful man works so hard to provide and take care of me, and include me in his world, and did not truly deserve my anger.

Because I know of John's family history, his sense of duty and responsibility, and love him, I never want John or his inner child to feel unloved or unappreciated. I want his inner child to feel happy, relaxed, unburdened and carefree. I want John to be free from scolding and criticism. And when I hold that in my mind and heart, it motivates me to regulate my emotions and engage in relationship repair with sincerity and ownership of my part.

If you took the inner child perspective with your partnership, imagine what could unfold. I recently had a beautiful realisation in a session with a couple when reviewing how their conflict escalates. She criticises; he defends himself. Inside, she is feeling dejected and hurt by his anger and he is feeling not good enough. In other words, her inner child is feeling unloved and unseen by his response; his inner child is feeling angry and worthless.

In conflict, there is an internal battle for the individual. The battle is between the inner child and your healthy adult part; do you continue to lash out and express hurt from inner child wounds, or turn to your adult logic and compassion? If your healthy adult can take over, you can acknowledge that your partner is hurting too and seek repair. It all starts with awareness and choosing compassion.

Couples and Compassion

Compassion must be the cornerstone of our relationships if they are to thrive. To know your inner child and care for them is self-compassion. To care for your partner and all their parts, is 'relational compassion'. Compassion can be more readily accessed when there is understanding and knowing. Compassion is about being able to extend forgiveness, patience, care and kindness to another because you know and understand their life experiences, wounds, feelings, and internal world, and therefore all their reactions and behaviours make sense. And, from compassion comes acceptance of another, as they are, without needing them to change.

I have seen compassion save relationships when it becomes a common practice (and it does take practice!). I have seen a wife able to let go of her anger towards her husband when she realised how much worry he was carrying for his extended family living overseas. I have seen a female partner forgive her male partner's early relationship betrayal because she understood it was related to his own mental health struggles and knows that today he is a man of integrity and honour. Their love is greater than one moment in time, and the act of relationship repair further solidified their love and commitment going forward.

Compassion makes our partner human and vulnerable. Couples therapy must often start with an acknowledgement that both partners are hurting, not one partner only. With compassion for your partner's pain, there is more hope and possibility of a way forward.

This may seem like a controversial thing to say, but any relationship hiccup, even the seriously big ones, such as betrayal, affairs and destructively critical words can be overcome with compassion and a hearty repair. And, of course, a trusted couples therapist can help you navigate this. My recommendation would be a couples therapist, such as myself, who is trained in Emotionally Focused Therapy for couples, or Schema Therapy for couples.

EXERCISE
Compassion As Your Compass

Take a moment to consider these questions, either by writing them down in a journal or just taking a moment to contemplate the answers:

What is it like for you to view relationship hiccups as normal?

What relationship hiccups do you expect to crop up for you?

When Will It Happen For Me

What are the elements of a good relationship repair?

Consider a past or current partner. What may their inner child wounds be?

How can you bring more compassion to your relationships?

CHAPTER FIFTEEN
Momentum and Milestones

For the first time in my life, I had found myself in a truly happy relationship that had the reality of a bright future. I was feeling proud of how far I'd come, and my inner child was becoming increasingly content and settled. My relationship was gathering momentum, and we continued to hit couple's milestones: meeting each other's friends and family, traveling together, and talking about our future.

At times, I felt like I needed to pinch myself to check it was all real. I was actually doing all the things that I'd watched other happy couples do with envy. And, whilst I was excited and confident in John as a partner, I also stubbornly told myself to be cautious.

I'd made a promise to myself to take things slowly this time because I had always rushed in every other relationship. I'd lived with partners or been engaged in a matter of weeks or months, and we all know how that went. But, as life would have it, I was faced with a conundrum.

I had been living on my own for less than a year. In fact, I had strategically locked myself into a one-year lease as I had decided that was the minimum time I should be living alone before I moved in with another person. I'd put a safeguard in place so as to avoid mistakes of the past. However, my home was becoming unliveable. Unfortunately, the apartment opposite me was infested with maggots and they were now inhabiting my place. I was becoming increasingly stressed about my dog's health and I was exhausted from battling the real estate agent to chase my landlord to fix it.

Throughout all this, John had been incredibly supportive, emotionally and practically, helping me with cleaning and being a listening ear. In the ideal world, I wanted to live out my lease, but it was becoming apparent, I needed to get out. I also didn't feel enthusiastic about moving again as that can be so stressful. In my mind, I intended for this apartment to be the last one where I'd be single, as I'd been so determined to heal and have my happily ever after.

I had many scenarios running around my mind. John and I had talked about living together eventually, but this certainly sped up the timeline. I wanted to be guided by my own intuition and healing at this fork in the road.

I also had the opposing voices of different, caring professionals echoing within me. I could hear my male psychologist in my head reminding me of my 'urge to merge.' I was all too aware of my fear of abandonment schema, and my tendency to rush to feel secure in a relationship. Yet, I also had a lot more confidence in myself than ever before and, underneath my fears, I knew that I was ready for more commitment, if need be.

I had joined a Schema Coaching group for female therapists. We met once a week online to discuss Schema Therapy and how we were integrating it into our work and personal lives. Their support gave me confidence in connecting to my healthy adult part and choosing a healthy relationship. Whilst caution was warranted, I needed to know that I could trust myself and my life decisions again.

In short, I was battling with myself. There was the protective part of me that was determined to be cautious and the 'knowing' part of me that knew my self-trust was restored. In reality, I didn't need to battle because, deep within, I had faith in myself again. Ultimately, this was another relationship lesson about the importance of being guided by your healthy adult part, listening to your own intuition, and going at the pace that feels right for your own relationship. Sometimes timelines shift because you do too.

And so, we agreed: we would move in together. As soon as the decision was made, I felt excited but oddly calm. This was not a decision that unsettled my nervous system. I knew my dedication to healing had helped me choose the right person. We both felt ready to blend our lives together.

If you are in tune with who you are, how you feel, and what you need, you'll be more able to live in alignment, rather than getting caught up in all the shoulds, musts, and rules that others live by or project on to you.

The Curse of Comparison

Comparison can be a destructive and powerful force, fuelled by social media and well-intentioned friends and family who may have a narrow definition of what a healthy relationship actually is. Your healthy relationship may look very different to another's healthy relationship. Thankfully, these views of what constitutes a normal, healthy relationship are changing. However, I still see the huge pressure placed on women in particular to partner up, move in, get married and then have kids. It's the expected natural order of things. I fell victim to this, just like my clients do.

I'm thinking of one female client who has incredible societal, cultural, familial, religious, and life-stage pressures upon her to marry her male partner as soon as possible. Despite these pressures, she first sought couples therapy with her male partner in order to overcome their patterns of conflict and restore emotional safety. Only then, will she say 'yes', she says. I have such admiration for her strength and courage to make her own rules for living rather than engage in comparison.

I believe, part of the reason I got my eggs frozen was due to the curse of comparison and the pressure for women to conceive and become mothers. I didn't really stop and have a deep conversation with myself about what I really did want for my future. And a part of the reason I felt shame and sadness for being single was comparing my relationship status and age to those of others.

My female clients, in particular, will come in and tell me how all their friends are now married and with children, how they feel on the outer and that they should be at the same stage. They battle grief and the curse of comparison. I often have to remind them that they are their own person; their childhood, temperament, career choices, and trauma have impacted their timing. And then we work on clarifying what they actually do want, rather than being guided by where they think they should be. We seek these relationship milestones, falsely believing that they will fill us up emotionally. The truth is, only a loving connection to yourself can do that.

You can overcome the trap of social comparison with some of these ideas:

Building Security In Love

- ♥ Limit your social media exposure and stop the scroll when you notice yourself comparing your life to that of an 'ideal'.
- ♥ Pause or mute certain accounts, pages, or friends if the curse of comparison is causing pain.
- ♥ Clarify what would *actually* make you happy (going back to your values can help with this).
- ♥ Create a more flexible definition of a life well-lived for you; one that extends beyond having a partner, kids, money, and marriage.
- ♥ Radically accept where you are at in life, and trust in the pace and timing of your life's journey.
- ♥ Remind yourself that it is both okay to want or not want a partner, marriage, and kids.
- ♥ If you are in a relationship, give yourself permission for your relationship to move at a pace that works for you and your partner.

If you can navigate and detach from comparing yourself or your relationship, you'll experience the freedom of living life at your own pace.

And if things are moving ahead with a partner, then it's important to ensure you're *both* going down the path you want to take. Many of us prioritise the feeling of love when we choose our partner, rather than looking at the reality of what your partner wants and assessing if your life directions match. Don't bypass the important step of talking the big things through.

Have The Big Conversations

A month before John and I moved in together, he raised the topic of finances and how we would manage life responsibilities. It could have been a heavy conversation but, to me, it was romantic; a sign of our ongoing commitment. I felt relaxed, knowing that John took an attitude of being a team. Fairness and equity were important to me given my history of self-sacrifice and relationship burnout.

I've worked with many couples who have committed to a life together *before* having conversations about big, important topics, including managing finances, the decision to have children, parenting, navigating in-laws and where to live.

Now I know the big conversations can be scary. Perhaps you are avoiding these big conversations because, in the past, they have brought up conflict and you couldn't come to an agreement. Or you fear realising that you would want different things, or you assume that love is enough to assure your happily ever after.

Sorry to tell you, this probably isn't going to cut it. If you want your happily ever after, sometimes love isn't enough. Aligned future values and goals are equally important.

The reality is that some couples commit to each other and then realise they want different things. We also evolve as people over time—that's natural and normal. You could both start out wanting the same thing and then that changes. Perhaps one partner hopes the other will change their mind and continues to wait for this day. How will you know, and be able to address it, if you avoid the big conversations?

I had spent much of my life believing I wanted kids and brought this up to John very early on in our relationship (probably within the first month or two). One evening, when we were at my place sitting on the lounge, he turned to me and told me that he had been thinking about children and realised that he didn't want them. He then listed his (very valid) reasons: largely that he felt, he couldn't be physically and emotionally available enough to them.

I have to say, it took me by surprise. And it left me in a possibly deal-breaking predicament. How much did I long for children and a family? Now that I'd found a loving partner, would that be enough for me? Could I commit to our relationship, and respect John's wishes, without hoping that I could change his mind in the future?

That evening, we circled around and around the conversation. We wanted each other to be happy; John didn't want to stop me having the life that I wanted. We also wanted to be together. We couldn't reach a conclusion in one evening, so we agreed to pause and sleep on it.

After John left the next morning, I felt very, very sad. It felt like I was losing him, and that our future was in jeopardy. I questioned whether we should continue in our relationship or end things. I was also shocked and panicked because our big conversation was unplanned. I thought we'd already had the 'baby conversation' when I raised it in the early stages of our relationship and now, here we were, having it again.

In the past, I would have distracted myself or fallen into unhealthy coping mechanisms. But, on this occasion, I just sat in the discomfort. I cried and journaled, and thought about the best parts of my relationship, and spoke with my wisest friend. And, within a few days, it became clear. I knew that having an emotionally available partner mattered to me most of all, and John is that. And I also realised that I'd probably idealised having kids and a big happy family because society pushes that dream upon women.

When Will It Happen For Me

With healing, something strange has happened to me. I'm no longer as strongly tied to meeting the life milestones of marriage and children as I once was. Healing can create ease in our lives. I suspect my inner child didn't feel alone anymore, and our current family is enough for her.

I know, I was lucky that my chat with John went well. My hope is that this example shows you the importance of having the big conversations early on, preferably planned. I could have easily made a very different decision, and ended our relationship, if I had panicked and reacted.

Only open communication will allow for each of you to remain informed and pursue the life you want. So, please slow down and spend some time with your partner to talk about your visions for the future, so that you can know if they align. Reflect upon how much you value your partnership versus the life milestones you long for.

So, in the spirit of being a healthy adult, here's how to have the big conversations.

- ♥ As soon as you realise that you're envisioning a realistic future with this person, mention this to them. You may say something like: *'We've been together a while now, and I'm thinking more about our relationship future. I think it's worth talking about the things we each want in our futures.'*
- ♥ Make a time to chat, each bringing a list of the important life milestones that matter to you. I've included a list at the back of this book to inspire your talking points (turn to page 240). Be prepared to open yourself up.
- ♥ Take some time to each reflect about how each other's

Building Security In Love

important life milestones align or contrast. Consider what are your 'musts' or areas of flexibility.
- ♥ If things become heated, slow down and consider if you'd benefit from a couples therapist who can help you clarify the relationship direction, and whether it's best to continue on or not. Some differences can be worked through, and others present insurmountable hurdles.
- ♥ Big conversations are not a one-and-done thing. Schedule a yearly review of the topics on the list and be open to how your views might have changed with life's seasons.

It's important to let the momentum slow down to truly assess. The life you want is in your hands, and I wish you the courage to go after it.

EXERCISE
Where Do I Want To Go?

Take a moment to consider these questions, either by writing them down in a journal or just taking a moment to contemplate the answers:

How has social comparison hurt you?

Write some ideas here for giving up comparing yourself to others (refer to page 193).

Building Security In Love

What relationship milestones matter to you?

What is your personal definition of a life well-lived for you; one that extends beyond having a partner, kids, money, and marriage? Dare to dream for yourself.

If you're in a relationship, what relationship values and milestones do you need to talk about? Consider how you may prompt the conversation with your partner.

CHAPTER SIXTEEN
Moving In

They say that moving is one of the most stressful things you can do, and that can be made tougher when couples move in together for the first time. As John and I prepared to move under the same roof, I was dealing with a lot of emotional challenges: an unreasonable landlord, an unkind real estate agent, and a maggot infestation, as well as worrying about my puppy adjusting to a new home. I certainly wasn't my best self.

John would later admit, he had his doubts after seeing my fragile emotional state during the move. I feel too embarrassed to reveal my exact behaviour here but let's just say, my inner child trumped my healthy adult on a few occasions. Luckily, we were able to repair and overcome this particular hiccup.

I think John saw that once the hurricane of moving had passed, I was a much more likeable human—the one he first fell in love with. And so, we eased into a new routine and life together, blending our busy careers and time with our puppy, adjusting to different sleep routines and Netflix preferences.

There were bumps that required smoothing out, like me struggling with John's different schedule and priorities. He can work a lot (up to eighty hours a week at times) and the state of his home office is simply not a priority. And that, coupled with my tendency to over-extend myself and self-sacrifice, meant that, without thinking, I started doing chores to 'help him out'—and then I became resentful. John was grateful when I did his laundry at first, which made me feel good for a while, but soon I was tired from the extra work, and there was a growing sense of unfairness.

One thing I had worked on in Schema Therapy is knowing that resentment has no place in a relationship. If you don't stop, listen to your feelings, and self-reflect, your schemas can be triggered in your new relationship outside conscious awareness and risk turning a happy relationship sour.

The Blending of Worlds

Moving in with a partner can feel scary for a lot of us. In living with a partner, they are exposed to the 'real you'. There may be fear of it not working out, that they won't like the real you, that you're committed forever, or you will end up just like your unhappy parents. You may worry that you'll feel trapped, that your life will shrink, or you'll lose your freedom and yourself in the process. Ultimately, the decision to move in together should feel like it will add to or enrich your life.

There is both more and less intimacy as you move in together. You tend to grow in closeness and share more time together, yet there is also a risk of losing the excitement and joy of the honeymoon phase, as you now share the unromantic task of domestic responsibilities.

You may forget to nourish and nurture your relationship with dates, quality time, romance, and bonding conversations. It's a big transition and yet one we're often not emotionally prepared for. And if we're not careful, our schemas can take over and our same old dysfunctional relationship patterns repeat.

Those Sneaky Schemas

The most common schema I see triggered in a relationship when couples move in together, is self-sacrifice, particularly for women. Being driven by our deep longing for love, we give and take on whatever we can to make our partner's life easier.

My self-sacrifice schema was activated with John, and I didn't even notice it happening at first. My resentment was a big clue that this schema was still running my life. Importantly, John never asked me to take on his laundry; I just did it automatically. My schema made me do it.

Here are some other common patterns of relationship behaviour pointing to schema activation, especially when blending two worlds and living together:

- ♥ **Emotional Deprivation:** If you have this schema, you are at risk of feeling unloved, unseen and unnurtured. If you have come to expect this from others, you are not likely to ask for the love and care you need from your partner, and hope for them to read your mind. As you transition to moving in together you may feel less loved and nurtured due to a shift in the couple dynamic from initial bliss and dates to domesticity.

When Will It Happen For Me

- ♥ **Fear of Abandonment:** Living together is stressful, and normal conflict can feel overwhelming if you have this schema. You may worry that fights are severe and threatening, rather than part of the process of adjusting to stress and a new milestone. When triggered, it risks sending you down an anxious spiral.
- ♥ **Subjugation:** Relationship peace may be your priority and stop you being assertive with your partner in order to avoid conflict or retaliation, and so you may find yourself going along with their needs. They may start to feel your internalised resentment, which you may even deny.
- ♥ **Approval-Seeking:** Wanting your partner to like you or view you as kind and good may prevent you from raising concerns and eventuate in you minimising your needs in a shared home.
- ♥ **Defectiveness and Shame:** If you have a shaky base of self-worth, your partner's low mood or irritation after a hard day of their own may be taken personally. Often couples living together absorb the emotional energy of the other or assume responsibility for their partner's happiness at home. People-pleasing, excessive empathy or over-extending oneself can take over in order to manage this shame.

In our next section, 'let's get practical', I give a four-step process for getting your relationship back on track when these schemas are activated after moving in together.

Many of these schema patterns and behaviours contribute to resentment building and require action in order to restore a new balance. You can overcome these traps by expressing your emotional needs and believing that your partner wants to support you, trusting in the permanency of the relationship and your commitment to talk things through, negotiating relationship boundaries, and speaking up sooner rather than later.

Don't Let Resentment Fester

Anger and resentment are the most destructive relationship emotions and the antidote to this is airing frustrations immediately. I learnt this in my therapy journey, and it has saved my relationship and those of my clients many times over.

Most co-habiting couples arrive to my office when the resentment feels almost insurmountable. Typically, a self-sacrificing female partner has been carrying the mental load of the household and is quite simply over it. Her partner, however, is not solely to blame. Often, she has kept quiet because she had tried and tried to express her needs, and it only got her so far. Maybe initially there's change, and then it goes back to how it was. By the time the couple arrives at therapy, it's nearly too late. So, I caution you: please don't be the partner who gives up communicating their needs. And please don't be the partner who doesn't take your partner seriously enough and action change.

Let's Get Practical

Although the enthusiasm of a new chapter of moving in together can be overshadowed by these moments, it doesn't have to be.

When Will It Happen For Me

There are ways forward to restore contentment on the home front. It all goes back to being a healthy adult.

In my opinion, being practical when it comes to love is not unromantic, it is necessary to fuel ongoing romance, play, and couples connection. And it is particularly important in the busyness and chaos of living together. Part of being a good partner is making a plan to restore connection when things feel off.

Here are some pointers to get your relationship back on track when you're living together:

- ♥ **Understand How You Feel:** If you notice something feels 'off' in your relationship, spend some time understanding your emotions and what they're communicating. For example, perhaps you're over-functioning, not feeling appreciated or missing the earlier days of your relationship.
- ♥ **Speak Up:** Commit to being the type of partner that doesn't let things fester inside, but raises matters in a gentle and timely manner.
- ♥ **Ask For What You Need:** Do trust that your partner equally longs for connection, and ask for that. Express to your partner how they could make you feel more loved.
- ♥ **Nurture The Couple:** With your partner make a commitment to more actively nurture your relationship. This may include scheduling in more intimacy, regular date nights, or a weekly walk where you can simply talk.

I often marvel at the couples who do it well. Despite all the relationship knowledge and support that exists, I often find myself thinking no wonder couples run into trouble—two individuals with different upbringings, cultures, attitudes, and relationship histories are trying to find harmony in the face of these differences. So, let's turn to one more important couple obstacle to overcome that I see often in my practice.

Clashing Cultures and Extended Family

For me, it wasn't really until I moved in with John that I fully understood how our different cultures impacted our relationship expectations and approaches to family. John is of Asian descent and an eldest son, which carries certain responsibilities for him. His family migrated abroad in search of work, education and economic security. John's family are warm and there was no shouting in his home, ever.

I am of Australian background and have never felt responsible for my family in the way that he does; his gratitude to his parents for giving him access to a better life defines his outlook on life. And there was a lot of shouting and emotional expression in my home. My emotional sensitivity, irritability, and fiery expression has shocked John who only knew calm, kind and regulated conversations. Talking our backgrounds over has reminded us of our differences and allowed us to translate each other's actions.

I have witnessed culture clashes in my client couples, which become particularly apparent as they embark on having children. They can no longer just be a couple because they're navigating a blending of two family systems, cultures and religions. My clients are from a variety of religious and cultural backgrounds, including Christianity, Judaism, Islam, and diverse cultural traditions from Australia, China, India, Europe, and South America. And I always have an open approach to learn about my client's cultural backgrounds, and ask curious questions in order to understand the beliefs, expectations, and pressures that each individual within the couple may face.

Some partners may long for more separation from their family of origin, whilst other partners long to maintain a greater closeness to their family of origin. This longing can either be their own or the pressure they experience from their family.

These cultural differences have showed up in my therapy room around expectations for raising a child, and child-minding in particular; one partner longs to put their child into day care to give their child social connections, whereas the other partner longs for their parents to fulfill the caring role. This difference can be an even greater source of tension for a couple who have been in conflict for a long-time, as their sense of warmth and trust in each other is eroded. I believe a couple committed to restoring relationship security can work through these issues.

Here's how I would help any couple navigate this situation:

- ♥ **Restore emotional connection first:** a couple will be more able to discuss matters of culture, extended family, and priorities when there is a strong emotional connection. Work on de-escalating conflict, trying to see your partner's perspective and longings, and validate their feelings, even if you see things differently.
- ♥ **Stay curious:** ask your partner about their hopes to include their family in your life. You may discover a greater meaning behind this longing.
- ♥ **Cultivate compassion:** have conversations about each other's upbringing, connection to extended family, gender roles, views on finances, children and childcare.

Building Security In Love

Understanding fosters compassion and allows you to not take things personally.

- ♥ **Try to find the good in your partner:** behind the conflict is a person with their own story and longings, who likely doesn't mean to hurt you, but is trying to juggle maintaining connection to you and their family of origin.
- ♥ **Prioritise the couple:** as much as there may be extended family to please and include in your life, the couple unit and your partner's happiness must be a priority. I aim to be culturally sensitive and appreciate the value of grandparents and extended family, however, parenting decisions should be agreed upon by both members of the couple and communicated to extended family as the decision of the couple. You should be a united front to the outside world.
- ♥ **Allow for individuation:** there may be times when there is conflict between one partner and their partner's family. Sometimes, limiting interaction is healthy and supports the preservation of the relationship. This comes back to avoiding comparing to other couples and how they navigate family. You must do what you find best for your unique situation.
- ♥ **Sometimes family doesn't know best:** unfortunately, I meet couples where their extended family cause havoc in their lives. Some parents' behaviour can be emotionally manipulative, mean, exploitative, and damaging. To get an accurate gauge on this, you may need to seek therapy. Boundaries, including no contact, may be the best course of action for dealing with a toxic family member.

EXERCISE
Moving in, Moving Forward

Take a moment to consider these questions, either by writing them down in a journal or just taking a moment to contemplate the answers:

Which of your schemas are at risk of being activated upon living with a partner?

How do you manage these schemas and restore relationship health?

How can you keep romance alive and nurture your relationship after moving in?

Building Security In Love

What matters of culture do you need to consider in your relationship with a partner?

What issues do you need to talk about regarding extended family and expectations? Write any tips here to set this conversation up for success.

CHAPTER SEVENTEEN

Separateness Versus Togetherness

In my relationship, there are still times when I struggle with balancing our differing needs for separateness and togetherness. John is often incredibly busy with work and study. He has had many overseas and domestic work trips, and it has its challenges. This often means that he needs to catch up on rest and I sometimes don't have a 'present partner'. He also has friendships to nurture and needs time alone to decompress, being an introvert.

We have had to find the balance of alone time, and couple time, to meet each of our individual needs. At first, I found the amount of time we spent apart tough. I knew, however, that I would need to find a way to make peace with it (and even feel grateful for it). John's work matters deeply to him, and John matters deeply to me, and so we work on it.

I'm quite sure that being able to tolerate this separateness has been made possible due to the healing work of connecting to and soothing my inner child. I have been pleasantly surprised how I have thrived with distance, and have come to enjoy my own space and time.

When Will It Happen For Me

I have seen couples break up for failing to strike this balance when one partner's need for closeness means that a partner doesn't get their need for separateness met. Schemas such as dependence/incompetence, emotional deprivation, enmeshment, and fear of abandonment can unconsciously drive us to rely on our partner for connection, thereby risking their happiness and that of the relationship. Alone time provides the space to decompress and to be your most authentic self, which is essential to our wellbeing.

There's essentially no one-size-fits-all approach to this common problem. The answer is to listen to your own feelings to guide your needs and come up with a compromise together.

In my own journey, I have learnt that the quality of togetherness is more important than quantity. When we are together, if we talk and share our emotional worlds with true presence, my emotional needs are met. I have noticed that the same is often true for the couples I work with who also have busy lives, careers, and are juggling the pressures of being parents and carers.

When there is a secure attachment within a relationship, there is a deep trust, whereby you feel able to observe your partner go out into the world and thrive, knowing that they will return back to you—their secure base. The bond of secure attachment facilitates separateness and supports the growth of both individuals in the couple.

In separateness, you can check in with your emotions and energy levels, and then meet your needs. In the space, you can engage with your own interests, hobbies, and friendships that differ to your partner. Space can be truly restoring and nourishing, and allow you to bring the best of you back to the relationship. It is important to have regular, ongoing discussions as a couple about your needs for separateness and togetherness, and I encourage you to use the time apart to work on connecting to yourself (and your inner child).

Remember that you alone cannot meet your partner's needs, nor can they meet all of your needs. A healthy couple benefits from the support of the community around them.

It Takes A Village

In an often frantic world, our friends, family, and community can be lifesaving. Along the journey from singledom to partnership, there is tremendous support to be acquired from fellow female friends who just 'get' the challenges of relationships.

And when it comes to being in a couple whether with or without kids, having a village of support matters. There are many members in our village—our doggy day-care sitter, our extended family, friends, our gyms, my Italian teacher, our therapists, colleagues, and baristas, to name a few. They all support and nourish our soul in unique and important ways to help us be the best versions of ourselves, so that we can keep showing up for each other. A healthy couple is made up of two healthy individuals, each accessing their support systems.

During my single past, I often longed for more connection, as I wrote about earlier on. Looking for love, navigating dating, and having a deep longing for partnership can feel isolating, particularly if those around you are partnered up or not at all interested in finding love. Running into relationship troubles can feel equally isolating or even shameful, and you may struggle to open up to your family and friends. I knew there had to be a better way.

Part of why I wrote this book and developed my women's

healthy relationship group program, *The Complete Toolkit For Dating and Maintaining Love* is that I never wanted another woman to feel alone in her healing journey, whether dating or in a committed relationship.

I never wanted another woman to feel ashamed about what point she was at in her relationship journey. I wanted every woman to know there is a clear pathway to healing wounds that block us giving and receiving love. I wanted every woman who longs for love to have hope in finding it. I wanted every woman to have access to her own village of support. What I didn't know when I started running these groups was just how powerful they can be. These women become each other's mirrors, supports, cheerleaders, and friends.

To find out more about my women's group and the course, visit my website
www.therelationshipspace.com.au.
I'd love to see you there.

In my course, we cover all the key topics to help women find and keep love: understanding your family of origin story, relationship values, love languages, dating and red flags, emotional maturity, navigating insecure attachment, vulnerable communication, healing, connecting to and soothing your inner child, overcoming shame and the inner critic, and cultivating more self-love. I now run this online group several times per year, and have been moved by the power of vulnerability of these groups.

These women have healed themselves and each other by being open, real, raw, and honest. When one woman shares her story, another hears parallels to her own story—a story of abandonment, neglect, rejection, or emotional deprivation. These parallels exist regardless of age, sexuality, culture, relationship status. I intentionally developed this group for all women, whether single or partnered, because whatever relationship stage you're at, the healing work is often the same: to cultivate more self-awareness and a more deeply loving connection to yourself.

Shame is overcome through the power of sharing, which normalises and humanises each experience, and creates a sense of connection, solidarity, trust, and community. Welcome to a group of women whose vulnerability and courage spurs on the healing of one another. When one woman bravely pursues online dating, another woman feels more inspired to do the same; or when one woman starts opening up to her partner like never before, and their connection grows, other women are filled with hope for their relationship future.

The women in my groups have moved and astounded me in the way that they have shared and bared their souls. They have reflected upon their inner child story, and shared their new dialogue with their inner child, radiating greater self-compassion and love. The most common word they tell me is that they feel 'empowered'—to soothe their inner child, overcome triggers, and to speak their truth. And as these women evolve, so too do their relationships, for the better. And future generations heal.

EXERCISE
My Needs, Your Needs, Our Relationship Needs

Take a moment to consider these questions, either by writing them down in a journal or just taking a moment to contemplate the answers:

What are your personal needs for separateness and togetherness? Consider the same for your partner.

If you struggle with separateness, write down the possible benefits of more space in your relationship.

Building Security In Love

What current supports make up your village and strengthen your relationship? What supports would you like to build further?

CHAPTER EIGHTEEN
Starting Over (Again)

As I sit in our home, writing the final chapters of this book on a Monday morning, it is grey and overcast outside. I can hear the cracking sounds of thunder followed by pounding rain, but our home is a place of warmth. My heart is at ease, and I am in my safe place. We have now been living together for just over a year, and I feel proud of us, as individuals and a couple.

My favourite part of the day (and I'm sure it is John's too) is our morning walk with our beloved toy Cavoodle, Bella, and grabbing a coffee from the café on the corner. It centres and grounds me for the day, and I love that he shares his stresses and thoughts with me. I share my work ventures and ideas with him. I feel more confident than I ever have, personally and professionally, and a huge part of that is due to John.

I often marvel at who John has become. I remember my nerves when I first let John take Bella's dog leash on our first walk after we had moved in together. He had grown up with dogs and was yet to take a very active interest in Bella. Fast-forward almost two years later, and he is besotted with her. She has become daddy's girl, and he is her favourite of the two of us. He is the first person she greets when we return home, and she can often be found sitting on the stool under his work desk. Their growing bond has been the most beautiful thing to witness.

John's warmth, emotional expression and affection towards me has also grown exponentially. He is an updated version of the person I first fell in love with. He has these added relationship qualities that have contributed to him evolving into an even more incredible partner and dog dad. As I've said earlier, I think that's the point of being in a relationship—that your partner enriches your life, and you enrich theirs.

For me, John has become a steady force and cheerleader. He always believes in me as I take on new professional challenges (including writing this book!), and he is an advocate for my emotional self-care. The security he has provided has fostered a fierce confidence and independence within me.

In such a short space of time, we're both different people than when we first met. I think we're updated and improved versions of who we were, with new boundaries, styles of communication, future visions, dreams, career aspirations, longings, hopes, and temperaments. We each need different levels of emotional closeness and space. I observe this evolution in most couples I work with. The challenging part of a relationship is, you fall in love with this person but, if you are together for an extended length of time, they will change and evolve, and you will have to fall in love with that person and, hopefully, fall in love with the newer version of them.

Within relationships we adjust, grow, and change. And with increased emotional safety, you both become more free to be yourself. All parts of you are welcome, even the parts that may hurt, upset, or shock your partner. And that's when staying together becomes a renewed choice; a commitment to accept and love your partner as they evolve.

Falling In Love With Every Version Of Your Partner

Here are some of the ways in which partners evolve over time that I have witnessed, professionally. Often couples come to therapy not because they are incompatible, but because they're going through growth, and their relationship is struggling to adjust to it. Here are some common growth hurdles I see in relationships:

- ♥ One partner may feel stagnant in life, or that they've lost connections over the course of the relationship and seek new challenges, hobbies, friendship circles and adventures, as most of their energy was directed inwards, towards the relationship.
- ♥ One partner may initially try to blend in with the friendship circle of their partner, but then deeply miss their roots and try to seek that connection.
- ♥ One partner may go to therapy and heal their wounds, and in turn grow apart from their partner.
- ♥ One partner may no longer be able to tolerate a lack of emotional connection, perhaps whilst their partner continues to be absorbed in their career growth.
- ♥ One partner may continue to focus their energies on parenting whilst the other feels a pull towards embracing their own needs.
- ♥ One partner may experience new found confidence and

connection to their body or sexuality and seek more intimacy.
- ♥ One partner may feel frustrated with city life and seek the slow pace of the countryside, whilst the other is not ready to leave it all behind.
- ♥ Or perhaps you try to fall pregnant and struggle for so long that it changes how you feel about having children, and it changes your partner too.

And then we age—we prioritise or neglect our fitness, fall into slumps, experience and overcome mental health struggles, lose self-esteem or gain confidence, lose and gain friendships, go through career burnout and re-evaluation, and wonder what life is all about.

One couple I worked with discovered they had vastly different approaches to health during the pandemic and struggled to connect as they each became opposingly different and alienated to each other. It was like one day they woke up and didn't know each other anymore. That couple made it through with therapy, compassion and increased vulnerability, and are stronger than ever. They chose to keep loving each other as they each became different versions of who they were. Their love was a choice to accept one another through this evolution, and was a privilege to witness.

The one certainty of partnership that is guaranteed yet rarely talked about is that you will both change. The experience of life and living changes us—hardships, failures, and struggles reveal new perspectives, often resulting in updated priorities, needs, boundaries, greater assertiveness, and an inner confidence from knowing you made it through and trust yourself more than ever before. I wonder if you could continue to choose your partner in the face of such growth.

Here are my tips for continuing to love in the face of change:

- ♥ Start with truly understanding the story of how your partner came to be as they are now—reflect on how life has changed them and see if you can access some compassion for their journey.
- ♥ Name the qualities that remain, which you continue to love, admire, and respect.
- ♥ Name the qualities that have updated and developed, and see if you can feel warmth towards their growth.
- ♥ Remember that true love requires acceptance for who you are, so try to avoid any agenda to change your partner.
- ♥ Do seek professional support if you are struggling to navigate these differences.

The Other Happy Ending

Although I'm ending this book in a relationship with a loving partner, it would be remiss of me not to cover the 'other' happy ending—the choice to leave a relationship that is no longer working for you, or the decision to stay single because your life is full and happy. Maybe you're reading this book at the end of a relationship, and you're still in a season of recovery. I don't want to end this book by saying 'here is my happy ending because I found someone.' No, my happy ending was doing The Work on myself, and reconnecting to my healthy adult. It was also realising, what a gift it was that my earlier relationships hadn't worked out. In another version of reality, I could still be in that space: sacrificing myself for another person who wasn't right for me.

So, let's talk about the other happy ending—leaving a relationship that isn't right for you.

There were many reasons to leave my last miserable relationship, but I'll never forget the feeling of finality and clarity when my ex-partner blatantly refused to engage in any couples therapy, or even return to individual therapy. This clear symbol of a lack of accountability and team work was all I needed to propel my decision to leave. I am now so grateful that this moment was part of my story. Every decision put me on the path to where I am today, and I truly believe that every part of my journey was necessary. Without immense pain and loss of love, I wouldn't have ended up where I am. Without courageously pursuing a healthy love, I wouldn't have met my person.

I left many, many dead-end, toxic relationships, and said goodbye to many unhealed partners, because each time I chose me. Each time I was prepared to face the anxiety of being alone, rather than staying in the despair of a dysfunctional and miserable relationship. And, in my more recent dating past, I chose to exit early on if our values weren't aligned or connection wasn't there. I listened to my feelings, needs and intuition in guiding me towards a better match.

I know the courage it takes to start over, from my professional and personal experience. One thing I do know is that starting over is possible at any stage and you're definitely braver than you know. Let's have a look at how to start over at any point, whether dating or questioning leaving a long-term relationship.

Should I Stay Or Should I Go?

Grappling with whether or not to end a relationship can feel overwhelming. It can feel particularly hard if there's still love for your partner, or if children are involved. It can also feel scary to leave a relationship if you're worried about the amicability of the separation, you feel trapped, guilty for leaving, or anxiety about your future. But you also shouldn't be fooled into thinking that things in your relationship will get better with time. I am often saddened and feel regret for a couple who come to therapy after living in a state of unhappiness for years. A skilled couples therapist should be able to tell you what can be worked on, and the process involved.

Here are some principles I've discovered working with couples for the past few years. When in doubt, seek therapy as soon as possible.

When couples therapy works well:

- ♥ **Both of you are open to the process:** couples therapy requires you both being willing to be vulnerable and committed to engaging in the process. You must do the work.
- ♥ **You're able to tolerate feedback:** you are willing to sit and hear your partner provide feedback about your behaviour, and the impact of this on them.
- ♥ **You're able to regulate your emotions, particularly anger:** a therapist can help you soothe your emotions so that you can share your inner feelings.
- ♥ **You're willing to do your own healing work:** you understand that doing inner healing of your own will benefit your relationship with your partner.

When Will It Happen For Me

A word on Emotional and Physical Abuse: *If you (or someone else) are in immediate danger, or if you have been threatened, physically hurt or sexually assaulted, you may need to call triple zero (000), consider speaking to Police, or seek support from a suitably trained professional. If physical or emotional abuse is recurrent, you feel unsafe and there is no remorse, shame, apology, and help-seeking, then seek professional help to know the true likelihood of change, to develop a safety plan, and work towards leaving this situation as soon as possible.*

If the issues you bring to couples therapy are significant, chronic and entrenched, you must know that couples therapy could take a long time. Sometimes individual therapy is also required, particularly if there are underlying mental health issues and unhealed trauma. An important part of my process is the assessment of the couple, including their own backgrounds and family histories, trauma, mental health diagnoses, attachment styles, and conflict dynamics. And another important part for me is informing the couple of the process of couples therapy. If there is complexity present, the process can be long and hard.

I really want couples to think this bit over: do you really have the energy and stamina to participate in this process? Do you have the emotional strength and support to go through a challenging and vulnerable process? I want you to know that it's okay to choose walking away. It is okay to choose your own happiness, even if that means starting over.

I also deeply hope that you walk away from your relationship knowing that you it gave all that you could. And I hope that you do the work required to heal any wounds that have blocked you from giving or receiving love and having a healthy relationship.

Building Security In Love

I hope, this book is step one for you in rediscovering your ability to love (yourself!). So, you can more confidently start again, when it comes to finding and keeping love—if that is what you choose for yourself.

EXERCISE
Holding Hope

Take a moment to consider these questions, either by writing them down in a journal or just taking a moment to contemplate the answers:

How have you evolved in your relationship journey?

If you have a partner, how have they evolved across your relationship?

Building Security In Love

What could you do to be more accepting of relationship growth and change?

What are the biggest relationship lessons here for you?

What experiences and learnings give you hope on your journey?

When Will It Happen For Me

Write a message to yourself here that can help you hold on to hope, and trust in your ability to heal and have the relationship you desire.

EPILOGUE

Love Isn't Perfect

As I'm preparing to write this final section, I answer a phone call from a dear colleague and friend, who is also a therapist. She wants to consult about a couple she is working with—and then she asks me about John.

My friends and very trusted colleagues know my story—the story of the kind-hearted sensitive friend, who had her heart broken many times and struggled in love. The empathic psychologist and couples therapist who so desperately longed for her own love story. When my friend asked how John was, I could answer with total honesty: 'He's great. Things are going really well. I can't believe how much we laugh together.'

As I write this, I know I'm exactly where I'm meant to be. Life really does have a funny way of sorting itself out. My job has healed me, and I have healed my inner child. My love for her knows no bounds, and I can finally trust myself again. Sometimes warmth radiates in my heart, and tears of joy find me because I'm so grateful for my life, my work, my loving friends, colleagues, and wise mentors who have crossed my path—all at the very right time.

When Will It Happen For Me

Most of all, I am grateful to John, for showing me how a reciprocal love feels, second only to Bella, the toy Cavoodle, whose love is unconditional.

I have learnt a lot about love in my time on this planet, and most of all I have learnt that love isn't perfect, nor should we expect it to be. The healed version of me realises, my expectations of love from others were too much in the past, as I sought love more from the outer world than from within. I now see gestures of love more clearly, and can more lovingly understand that others must meet their own needs first, and this allows them to show up with love.

My love story isn't perfect. My relationship isn't perfect, and nor is our love. John and I love in very different ways; sometimes, we can both struggle to be fully present to the other and sometimes we forget to nurture the relationship. When we fight, which is rare, we both hurt. And, whilst there is a deep trust in our future, there are no guarantees of a forever. But that is empowering because it means, I'll keep doing the work that it takes to be a kind and loving partner, as will he.

In our moments of disconnection, I know I can now rely on me. I will be able to soothe and comfort myself, and offer myself love, connection, and compassion in times of need. I know, I will never be alone and trust I can get through whatever hardships life throws at me. This is the beauty of inner child work. You are all you ever need; you are enough.

Wherever you're at in your relationship journey, whether single, navigating dating, considering ending a relationship, or feeling disconnected to your partner, I want you to know that it's all going to be okay.

With every bump in the road, if you can embrace an attitude of learning and growth, your inner strength will blossom. If you

Building Security In Love

have done the inner work of healing, and truly getting to know, comfort, and love your inner child, I know that you will be able to manage whatever life throws at you. There's a healthy adult taking care of your heart, always.

By learning to validate your emotions, nurture and comfort yourself, and speaking lovingly to yourself, you will have developed a template for a healthy, loving relationship. You will know how love feels. That's the wisdom of healing—when we love ourselves more, we trust in our intuition and decisions, and can bring more love and joy to our relationships. We can back ourselves to start over again at any point.

Please also know that you don't need to be perfectly healed to find and keep love. It is an ongoing journey for us all. And you certainly don't need to be the perfect partner. You're human, and we all have our wounds to bare. My hope for you reading this, is that your wounds receive the love they need, and that you keep learning to love.

And, if you're craving more support, I have free downloads and resources available on my website, including more information on Schema Therapy, my intuitive dating journal for empathic women within my *Roadmap to Love course,* and an invitation to join one of my women's healthy relationship group programs, *The Complete Toolkit For Dating and Maintaining Love.* I'd love to see you there—it's a beautiful group of women supporting each other with zero judgement.

Do I worry about being seen as the relationship therapist who struggled to find love? Not at all. In fact, I think it's the most perfect way to describe myself, because it humanises the complexities of connecting with another person, and the vulnerability that even so-called experts can feel putting themselves out there.

When Will It Happen For Me

I knew when I began writing this story that, even if I was single at the end of this book, it would be valuable and inspiring, relatable and useful to any other person who is navigating the world of relationships.

We all want to feel loved, whether it's from a romantic partner, our friendships, family or chosen family or community. I hope this book helps you to open your heart, and find the perfect love for you—especially from yourself.

Phoebe. x

APPENDIX
Extra Resources

Connecting With Your Inner Child

I believe that inner child work has the most significant healing power. Here's some inner child prompts that you can use to help you visualise her, and reflect on meeting her emotional needs. You can use a journal to write whatever comes up for you in response to the prompts below.

> *Get into a comfortable position, then close your eyes. Let go of any tension in your body; release the tension in your shoulders, your neck, your jaw, your forehead. Focus on the in and out movement of your breath, notice it's gentle rise and fall. Now open your eyes and write whatever arises for you.*

> *Imagine a time in the past. A time when you were younger, perhaps a child or a teenager. A time long ago, or even more recently that you sense is linked to your schemas.*

When Will It Happen For Me

A time where you may have felt rejected, excluded, abandoned, or not enough in some way. Perhaps your feelings were dismissed, or your need for emotional support was not met.

Try to bring to mind an image of younger you. If the image is fuzzy, or more of a feeling, that is okay. Just be present to whatever arises. You may notice where she is, what's happening for her, what her experience is.

Take in her posture, and expression, as if zooming in on her. Notice all that she may be feeling. Notice your inner child. You are taking her in, all of her feelings, and beliefs.

Write about what is coming up for you.

Next, imagine that healthy adult you is here for her now; imagine you stepping in to that image, however clear or otherwise. You are here to take care of her.

Let her know you see how she feels. Be curious about what's going on for her. Stay present to her. And because you know how she feels, you can take care of her.

Perhaps she needs reminding that things are not her fault.

Perhaps she needs company if she feels alone.

Perhaps she needs to hear that you see her worth and value.

Perhaps she simply needed you to check in on her.

Building Security In Love

Write about what your inner child needs from you.

Imagine what happens for her when she receives what she needs from you. Write about this some more.

Before you leave your inner child, gently consider if she needs any more from you, and if so, offer that to her. Trust that you know exactly what she needs. Write more if you need.

Remember that through your attunement to her feelings and needs, she will feel more safe and less triggered.

Slowly come back to noticing your breath, and your body. And write any further thoughts about this exercise.

If you feel emotional that is okay, or if you feel disconnected, that is normal too. Be sure to take care of yourself after this exercise.

The Big Conversations

Here's a list of talking points to review with your partner when things are becoming serious:

- ♥ where to live
- ♥ money matters
- ♥ co-habiting: when, how, and at what stage of your relationship
- ♥ owning property and how that would be managed, particularly if financial status and contributions differ
- ♥ your career aspirations and direction
- ♥ travel plans
- ♥ engagement and vision for a wedding
- ♥ marriage and what it means to each of you
- ♥ the decision to have children (naturally or via other means) and how you'd like to raise them
- ♥ monogamy, opening your relationship, sexuality and other preferences and needs

Acknowledgements

Different people had often told me that I was a good writer. I enjoyed writing reports for clients and synthesising ideas. A tarot card reader had once asked me about my writing. I had gone searching for answers and the meaning of life at many points in my past, during times of darkness; I saw tarot card readers, psychologists, studied countless courses and absorbed many self-help books. I am so profoundly glad that I found answers, and I am so proud to now call myself an author. I knew that there had to be better answers for my own romantic and relationship struggles, and I knew that other women would benefit from these answers too.

I have a deep appreciation for my work as a psychologist, it has made me a better, happier, and more healed person. To my clients, a heartfelt thank you for trusting me with your pain and vulnerability. You have made the most valuable contribution to my life; as I sit with you, I learn with you, and am filled with hope for humanity when each of you choose growth and healing. I deeply trust that in choosing my own healing I have enriched your lives.

To the women I've worked with, you may see a version of your story in these pages. Your stories matter and I know they will empower the reader to be as brave as each of you.

It is true that certain people come into your life at the right time and that is true with my editor, Amy Molloy—your gentle, clear guidance helped these pages shine; Amy connected me with my publisher, Natasha, at The Kind Press. Natasha, you made me feel safe and supported at every step.

To my first psychologist, Elizabeth; your humour, genuine care, and honesty live within me to this day, I am grateful to you.

To Tracey Hunter; your revolutionary work in Schema Therapy changed my life and relationship landscape; under your care I found love, and now teach these skills to my clients.

To my incredible colleagues and mentors, many of whom I consider close friends; I am so inspired by the work that you do, the world needs more humans like you. In particular, to Heidi—the most wise and caring friend, whose support is a true life line.

To mum and dad—you gave me the ability to dream and supported me to be myself. To my family, I love you.

To my loving partner—you are solid, reliable, calming, and I am a better person for having met you. You make our world a better place.

About the author

Phoebe Rogers is a Clinical Psychologist specialising in dating and relationships, a Couples Counsellor, and the Founder of The Relationship Space. She has helped thousands through her private practice, courses, and writing to transform the way they can romantically reset and find a loving relationship. Phoebe is sought out for her compassionate, direct, and integrative approach, using Schema Therapy, coaching, couples therapy, and good old-fashioned pragmatic advice. She also runs an online group for women who want healthy relationships.

For more support, discover free downloads and resources, including more information on Schema Therapy, the intuitive dating journal for empathic women within the *Roadmap to Love course*, plus an invitation to join the relationship group program, *The Complete Toolkit For Dating and Maintaining Love*: **www.therelationshipspace.com.au**

www.ingramcontent.com/pod-product-compliance
Lightning Source LLC
Chambersburg PA
CBHW031146020426
42333CB00013B/533